MONSOON ECONOMIES

History for a Sustainable Future
Michael Egan, series editor

Derek Wall, *The Commons in History: Culture, Conflict, and Ecology*

Frank Uekötter, *The Greenest Nation? A New History of German Environmentalism*

Brett Bennett, *Plantations and Protected Areas: A Global History of Forest Management*

Diana K. Davis, *The Arid Lands: History, Power, Knowledge*

Dolly Jørgensen, *Recovering Lost Species in the Modern Age: Histories of Longing and Belonging*

François Jarrige and Thomas Le Roux, *The Contamination of the Earth: A History of Pollutions in the Industrial Age*

Tirthankar Roy, *Monsoon Economies: India's History in a Changing Climate*

MONSOON ECONOMIES

INDIA'S HISTORY IN A CHANGING CLIMATE

TIRTHANKAR ROY

THE MIT PRESS   CAMBRIDGE, MASSACHUSETTS   LONDON, ENGLAND

© 2022 Massachusetts Institute of Technology

All rights reserved. No part of this book may be reproduced in any form by any electronic or mechanical means (including photocopying, recording, or information storage and retrieval) without permission in writing from the publisher.

The MIT Press would like to thank the anonymous peer reviewers who provided comments on drafts of this book. The generous work of academic experts is essential for establishing the authority and quality of our publications. We acknowledge with gratitude the contributions of these otherwise uncredited readers.

This book was set in Stone Serif by Westchester Publishing Services. Printed and bound in the United States of America.

Library of Congress Cataloging-in-Publication Data

Names: Roy, Tirthankar, author.
Title: Monsoon economies : India's history in a changing climate / Tirthankar Roy.
Description: Cambridge, Massachusetts : The MIT Press, 2022. | Series: History for a sustainable future | Includes bibliographical references and index.
Identifiers: LCCN 2021033921 | ISBN 9780262543583 (paperback)
Subjects: LCSH: Environmental policy—India. | India—Economic policy—1991– | India—Economic policy—Environmental aspects.
Classification: LCC HC440.E5 R69 2022 | DDC 338.954—dc23
LC record available at https://lccn.loc.gov/2021033921

10 9 8 7 6 5 4 3 2 1

CONTENTS

SERIES FOREWORD vii
ACKNOWLEDGMENTS xv
LIST OF ILLUSTRATIONS xvii
1 WHY CLIMATE MATTERS 1
2 WATER AND FAMINE 25
3 WATER AND EQUALITY 45
4 BECOMING A PUBLIC GOOD 65
5 WATER IN THE CITIES 87
6 WATER STRESS 113
7 SEASONALITY 137
8 MONSOON ECONOMIES 167

NOTES 177
SELECTED READINGS 203
INDEX 207

SERIES FOREWORD

The world is like the impression left by the telling of a story.
—Yoga-Vāsiṣṭha, 2.3.11

There is a certain banality to the now-commonplace assertion that the contemporary moment is one riven by extremes. The historian Eric Hobsbawm identified the short twentieth century, from 1914 to 1991, as the "age of extremes": a period of great creation and destruction, of massive social progress and repression, of rapid economic growth and collapse.[1] But while the extremes that typified Hobsbawm's reading of the twentieth century persist, the vantage point from the still-young century might want to impress greater emphasis on environmental extremes. Heat waves and droughts and wildfires and floods and rising sea levels serve as reminders that global climate patterns are tilting with ominous speed toward an ecological collapse that is threatening to surpass the economic collapses that Hobsbawm envisioned. The causes for Hobsbawm's age of extremes are tightly tied to this new period of ecological uncertainty, which the Indian novelist Amitav Ghosh has dubbed "the great derangement."[2] Nevertheless, it is difficult to imagine the kind of moment of clarity that could spark a global retreat from this psychosis or build an ark seaworthy enough to withstand this storm of progress. We continue to inhabit a world of extremes. "True hunger for extremity is rare," argues the writer and translator Laura Marris in a short and lovely essay on extremes. "Most animals that can temporarily survive in an extreme environment would prefer a less stressful one." Extremophilia—that hunger or love of extremes—is rare, in spite of Northern/Western academic fascination with extreme environments from the relative mundanity of climate-controlled offices. Human societies do not seek out extremes, but history says that they have frequently found ways to endure them. "Beyond extremophilia," Marris continues, "there is a second category: organisms that don't love extremes but manage to be exceptionally resilient."[3] Tirthankar Roy's *Monsoon Economies* offers an economic and geographic accounting of Indian resilience, through a region that is hotter, wetter, and drier than most places, and the historical challenges associated with navigating these very wet and very dry seasons on a warming planet. Indeed, the extreme heat experienced across much of the Indian subcontinent exacerbates the transitions between wet and dry seasons: heavy rainfall—so important for agriculture and survival—evaporates quickly, posing problems for its sustained use after the rains stop.

Readers familiar with United-Statesian inclinations toward boom and bust economies will identify some echoes in Roy's "monsoon economies." In this case, though, the extremes are driven by climatic and environmental conditions and demand much greater control over economic activities and resource use. These ecological variations provide valuable lessons for a world coming (much too slowly) to terms with resource scarcities.[4] Roy describes extreme seasonality and how monsoon dependency dictated seasonal work and (for many) seasonal poverty. Prior to 1900, economic insecurity and vulnerability across India (to say nothing of political disempowerment) meant that cyclical droughts and crop failures inflicted devastating famines, which killed millions—*millions*—of peasants.[5] After 1900, however, while seasonal extremes and cyclical droughts persisted, catastrophic famine diminished thanks to a series of evolving political, migratory, market, legal, and technological paradigms. Roy begins his narrative in 1880 and traces how the first steps in intensive agriculture and urban industrialization transformed both the Indian economic system and its relationship with drought, flood, and agriculture. In his introduction Roy translates this form of modernization in a manner that stuck with me: "Wider access to water [in India] . . . played as important a role in Indian economic history as fossil fuel extraction played in the economic emergence of western Europe." Water is the new oil is the new gold.[6]

The comparison is compelling, not least because historians of the global North/West pinpoint fossil extractivism as a critical chapter or turning point in a planetary environmental history. "Fossil capital" generated by this shift created copious (and concentrated) amounts of wealth while mortgaging the ecological future—and this is the crux of *Monsoon Economies'* place in this series, which explores the environmental past to better situate the future.[7] New water projects, before and after independence in 1947, initiated reclamation of marginal lands. The thrust of Roy's account is to interrogate how India managed to control the costs (monetary and in lives) of drought in spite of a heating region and world—and what that might mean if attention were projected forward to reflect on the environmental costs and the prospect of mounting conflicts. The uncomfortable lesson is that the radical overhaul of the subcontinent's water systems often rested on short-term exploitation of vulnerable water resources without any clear or sustained long-term vision as dams and reservoirs aged and aquifers dried up. In this work, Roy asks, "Who did water control work for?" The complex, historical answer makes for rich and rewarding reading. Irrigation projects and water recycling, storage, and distribution innovations witnessed a marked reduction in deaths from drought and famine, before and after independence, and a concomitant upward trend in economic growth. Independent India's first prime minister, Jawaharlal Nehru, lauded the construction of the Bhakra Nangal Dam (completed in 1963) as a "new temple of resurgent India," one of many expressions of a new high modernism that would see India into a prosperous future.[8]

At the same time, the value of *Monsoon Economies* isn't that it offers a(nother) reading of hubris and the winding road toward imminent apocalyptic environmental collapse. Instead, it highlights important ways of reflecting on the relationship between the histories of environment and economy to reach a better understanding of the present. Environmental and economic histories have traditionally worked at cross-purposes; too often these important fields talk past rather than to each other. Roy seeks to address that shortcoming by helping environmental historians to understand what they might learn and draw from comparative economic historians, while offering a vital water-centered environmental lens to help economic historians reorient their analyses. His story of Indian resilience is one that is forced to acknowledge multiple extremes. Parts of India are both very wet *and* very dry: monsoon economies represent a kind of three-body problem composed of metronomic extremes that put fundamental stresses on economies, agricultural regions, and human societies. This is an important history that Roy recounts with a deft touch, and he does it without losing sight of the contemporary implications of historical water control, acknowledging the gravity of the contemporary moment as a potential climatic tipping point. *Monsoon Economies* makes an important intervention in this series on history for a sustainable future precisely because of this vantage point. It embraces the series ideal that these short books should provide the present with historical perspectives that can inform future decision-making; in merging environment and economics, Roy injects two historical subdisciplines with valuable insights that will permit further cross-fertilization.

The transformation of water access/use in India and the engineering prowess involved (big and small) constitute another chapter in the *longue durée* of human civilizations resisting the limits imposed by the physical environment. At the risk of stripping the allegory of all its nuance, Barry Commoner's assertion that "there is no such thing as a free lunch" serves as a regular refrain in these histories.[9] But the stresses on India's water futures are real—and they pose uncomfortable prospects not just along ecological grounds. Geopolitical, too: the enduring tensions between India and Pakistan over Kashmir and between India and China—all three are nuclear powers—are grounded in competition over scarce water resources in a water-insecure region. But even without the border tensions, historical data and historical corollaries make for somber and sober reading. The rapidly shrinking levels of renewable water resources (Roy illustrates this in table 1.2) highlight the precipitous catastrophe that awaits India and many other tropical states. A further reminder, perhaps, that denizens of the twenty-first century should be wary—collectively so—of the Seneca effect, that notion that civilizational growth happens slowly, but civilizational collapse happens rapidly.[10] The dissonance between the speed of growth and the speed of collapse is yet another kind of extreme.

In her essay, Marris pivots from extremophilia to extremotolerance. From a love of extremes to tolerance of extremes, there emerges a growing resilience for societies and peoples inhabiting inhospitable landscapes. The story of water interventions in India over the course of the twentieth century is an exercise in developing resilience and tolerance. But tolerance comes at a cost, Marris warns: "For humans, tolerance is dangerous because you can passively persist in it while you wait for the world to change. Living in an air-conditioned apartment is a way of tolerating summers that get progressively hotter, distancing yourself from the physical effects of the heat, waiting for things to improve. And all the while, the ecosystem around you (your ecosystem) is facing the full force of those changes, year after year. While you enact your form of resilience and wait, other living things are becoming more stressed, and scarcer."[11] Tolerance of extremes might also lead critics and scholars to continue to ask the wrong questions and support it with the wrong data. What *Monsoon Economies* emphasizes to good effect is that sustainability metrics about consumption or greenhouse gas levels are less reliable categories of analysis in water-stressed environments. There is a marked danger that these entrenched ideals risk sacrificing the present in theory and in practice. Better, Roy teaches us, to look at the lessons that can be drawn from more stringent forms of cooperation and more effective forms of regulation at regional and state levels. What this history might also teach its diligent readers is to think about water not just as a historical phenomenon but also as a critical measure for reading the future.

Michael Egan

ACKNOWLEDGMENTS

The book emerged from a conference paper presented at Oxford University (New Approaches to the Global History of Capitalism) in September 2019. A short statement of the theme appeared in the *Journal of Interdisciplinary History* in 2020. I am grateful to all who commented on the work in its four incarnations: PowerPoint slides, working paper, journal article, and book manuscript. I particularly wish to thank the editor and the referees of the journal, and the three readers for the MIT Press who made many precise suggestions that led to significant improvements on the first draft of the book manuscript. Conversations with P. S. Vijayshankar on watershed management, A. Narayanamoorthy on drip irrigation, and Bharat Punjabi on cities made me more confident handling these topics. Anand Swamy made me aware of a limit of my argument. Jan Lucassen suggested a useful reference. Tim Goodfellow produced the maps. My warm thanks to all of them.

LIST OF ILLUSTRATIONS

Figures

1.1 Climate of South Asia excluding Nepal   9
1.2 Geographical zones, South Asia excluding Nepal and Afghanistan   10
1.3 Step well in western India   12
2.1 Rainfall in South Asia excluding Nepal and Afghanistan   28
2.2 Women and children collect water brought by train (June 2000)   33
5.1 Water tanker in a suburb   110
6.1 The Hirakud Dam   117
6.2 Drought in Marathwada   125

Tables

1.1 Water use, 1885–2015: Total and per head (annual)   16
1.2 Renewable water resource (cubic meters per head)   18

1

WHY CLIMATE MATTERS

Flood and famine are two aspects of one problem, development of the water resources of the country.
—National Planning Committee (India), 1947

Two recent media images of India's changing relationship with its environment are handy starting points for the book. A region notoriously susceptible to droughts and famines in the past succeeded in "drought-proofing" itself.[1] The anxiety about famines expressed in the 1947 report cited above remained powerful until the third quarter of the twentieth century. It started fading after that. The conditions producing droughts, heat waves, and weak monsoons did not disappear. On the contrary, global warming has made "deadly heatwaves the norm in India."[2] And yet, the degree of suffering from dryness fell over a century. Extraordinary achievements in water supply and distribution made the miracle possible. On the other side, in 2017 quietly and in 2020 noisily, India and China came to blows, stopping short of a full-scale border war. Control over the water of the Brahmaputra (Yarlung Tsangpo in Tibet and Jamuna in Bangladesh) is a source of constant unease in southern Asia. Demand for the river's water far exceeds supply, and "the potential for conflict between the world's two most populous countries over this finite resource is real."[3]

These accounts show us how deeply geography influences economic growth, welfare, and South Asian politics. They indicate that the impact is long-term, that it shaped the modern history of India, and that it creates enormous strains. A part of the narrative has an upbeat message, but another part is disturbing.

I explore the interaction between environmental change and economic change in India from around 1880 onward to find out why coping with nature has been a costly success.[4] I show that the tropical monsoon climate had made poverty and inequality in water access and extreme seasonal variations in employment universal conditions. From around 1880, steps taken to overcome these conditions began to succeed on an unprecedented scale. These steps led to mortality decline and population growth and encouraged intensive agriculture and urban industrialization. Water harvest and wider access to water, in this way, played as important a role in Indian economic history as fossil fuel extraction played in the economic emergence of western Europe. That extraordinary achievement, however, was bought at a price: environmental stress and political conflict.

The book will interest three types of readers. The first set consists of those attracted to the problem of explaining economic growth and inequality. Economic historians compare countries to discover the deep roots of economic growth in the modern world. They base most of their theories on the western European experience. These theories ask why the factors leading to the great economic transformation of nineteenth-century

Europe were missing from the rest of the world. The method is not reliable if world regions are incommensurate in their geographies. Because their initial conditions were different from those in Europe and North America, tropical monsoon economies could arrive at economic growth by solving different problems from those the Europeans and Americans needed to solve: ensuring reliable access to clean water and dealing with monsoon seasonality.

The second group the book aims to appeal to are readers interested in discussing the sustainability of economic change. The economic trajectory generates stress. Against the stress that it generates, is the economic pathway sustainable? What kind of interventions would make it sustainable? Answers to questions like these vary depending on what type of stress we are worried about, climate change or change in underground water stock.

My third target is those readers interested in the emergence of modern India. The British colonial empire established a rule over a large swathe of the region between roughly 1765 and 1947. The imperialists left a variety of legacies for the nations that emerged after 1947. The present political map of South Asia was one of the legacies. A great deal of the region's modern history studies the legacies and explains how nationalistic development policies reshaped them. In the process, historians get carried away and make too much of state power, whether the power of the British imperialist state or that of the nation-states. The book should be a corrective to that obsession with colonialism and nationalism when explaining the modern history of the non-Western world. In my account, which shows how geographical conditions influenced material life, power matters, but only because it had an indirect role in the basic process. The basic process is a form of environment-economy interaction.

* * *

Climate had a deep connection with poverty and inequality in India. What kind of connection? In the tropics, intense heat dries up surface water quickly, making mobilization of water for cultivation, industrial use, and consumption costly. In the monsoon tropics, the heat and the oceans also produce a powerful hydrologic cycle, making agriculture possible, but raising the risk of famines and floods. Economic shocks in South Asia were—and still are, to no small extent—environmental in origin. The climate caused drought if the monsoon was too weak and caused storm surges and floods if the monsoon was too strong. In the late nineteenth century, a succession of bad monsoons would raise prices, reduce consumption, raise debts, bring down banks. In the worst cases, there were famines and epidemic outbreaks among people weakened by malnutrition. In 1876, 1896, and 1898, famines hit peninsular India, killing millions. Droughts returned roughly once in seven years, always reducing consumption, sometimes causing severe stress to public finance, the balance of payments, and vulnerable communities.

In a "normal" year without floods or famines, farmers, laborers, and practically every other profession with a stake in land-based livelihoods had to deal with months of idleness. For monsoon dependency meant a short working season and a long stretch of the year too dry or too hot to conduct much business. During the slack season, those without assets and jobs reduced consumption and lived in poverty. The capitalists, such as bankers and moneylenders, withdrew from making investments to stay in readiness for the next busy season.

The extreme seasonality of the tropical monsoon, therefore, led to unemployment, poverty, and underinvestment.

From the time of the great famines of the nineteenth century, a deep-seated process of change set in. Famines disappeared in the region after 1900 (except one war famine in 1943), even though severe weather shocks persisted. Droughts became less destructive than before. Food production rose manifold. After the influenza pandemic of 1918 ended, the population growth rate, stuck at a near-zero average for forty years, started rising steadily. Some kind of intervention had eased the environmental constraints on economic change. What were these interventions?

The book shows that a characteristic feature of the changes was greater per head access to water and the availability of more water for communities earlier deprived. Although public works were an essential factor behind the change, the state was a limited agent. Popular politics, market forces, law, technology, and the knowledge gained in famine operations played significant roles. Greater water security enabled the reclamation of marginal lands, intensive agriculture, urbanization, and disease control.

Market forces also offered millions of people destined to be unemployed for a part of the year the chance to use their time better. Migration opportunities increased, thanks to the emergence of permanent worksites such as factories and plantations. New agricultural frontiers where canal irrigation enabled multiple cropping offered jobs to people so far dependent on rain-fed cultivation alone. As mobility and choice increased, rural employment contracts resembling bondage and serfdom crumbled. Migrants formed 2–3 percent of the population around the 1920s and 8–10 percent of those dependent on agriculture. The impact of mobility was larger than the numbers might suggest. Most migrants were the male members of a family. The family did not move. Still, the decision of some of its members to go changed the lives of those who stayed behind, if not always for the better.

Gaining security in a condition of absolute scarcity of renewable water, and, as I show, unstable river morphology, could not have come without negative consequences. Colonial India heavily used a state-led technological solution to water insecurity, impounding excess monsoon flow in rivers via dams, canals and reservoirs. In the twentieth century, the model came under intense criticism for the environmental and political costs it entailed and was effectively abandoned. As it became unpopular, users switched to groundwater. This second pathway changed the nature of the problem from insecurity to depletion of underground aquifers.

"India is in the grip of acute water scarcity," *BBC News* reported in August 2019.[5] That is not news to generations of Indians who struggled to overcome seasonal water shortages. Still, academic work on water tends to focus on the present and overlook history. Most scientists and economists today would see ecological stress as an example of the tragedy of the commons, wherein greed and unrestricted access lead to the degradation of shared resources. India's "crisis" is not a result of unchecked greed. It is instead a characteristic of the natural resource conditions of a tropical monsoon economy. The shaping of modern India is the story of a costly struggle to overcome an initial geographical condition.

* * *

The concept of the tropical monsoon climate needs a more precise definition. A good point to start is the Köppen-Geiger map of the world, which, using two dimensions, temperature and seasonality of precipitation, describes the climate of much of South Asia (as coastal West Africa and a part of Southeast Asia) as "tropical monsoon."[6] Tropical monsoon is a combination of two conditions, above-average temperature and seasonal concentration of rainfall. To illustrate the South Asian situation, I compare three climatic profiles, temperate, temperate monsoon, and tropical monsoon. An example of a temperate zone place is London. Tokyo is a temperate monsoon city. Delhi is a tropical monsoon city. In an average year, the maximum temperature in Delhi is about twice as high as that in London and 60–80 percent higher than that in Tokyo for every month of the year. The maximum exceeds 100 degrees Fahrenheit during the summer months in Delhi. In short, Delhi experiences aridity, whereas London and Tokyo do not. The three cities do not have significantly different average annual rainfall, but rainfall distribution over months in a year is skewed in Delhi and even or almost even in London and Tokyo. The monthly average rainfall in Delhi varies in a range of 10–250 millimeters, and 75 percent of the rains occur during the third quarter of the year. The monthly average rainfall is 40–70 millimeters in London and 50–150 in Tokyo. The seasonal concentration of moisture is a monsoon characteristic. Still, not all monsoons are alike. Delhi and Tokyo both have monsoons, but Delhi experiences aridity; Tokyo does not.[7] The tropical monsoon means a short season of comfort followed by a period of great aridity.

What does aridity mean? The heat in the tropical region dries up surface water. The average evaporation rate is a function of (among other variables) available surface water and the heat from the sun.[8] During summer in the Himalayas or the Arctic, the rate reaches high levels. In the deserts, the rate is low year-round. Any region with a high rate in one season and a low rate in another would have plenty of surface water in some months and lose it in certain other months. In most parts of India, the rate reaches 60–100 millimeters per month in June–September when the monsoon rain occurs in combination with high heat. As surface water dries up, the rate falls quickly. By April–June, the rate (0–20 millimeters) prevailing in nearly all of India except the Bengal delta and the southernmost regions of the peninsula such as Kerala tends toward the range that characterizes the great deserts of the Northern Hemisphere. The two figures on climatic zones (tropical savanna and desert and semiarid zones in figure 1.1) and rainfall patterns (figure 2.1) show the extent of the larger region's drylands.

The tropical monsoon limited the possibility of economic growth. Because surface water dried up quickly, agriculture and survival would require mobilizing water over long distances, mining it from below ground, or relying on the seasonally variable common sources. The first two options were expensive, and all three were uncertain because excessive heat reduced the infiltration and seepage that sustained nonsurface sources. Further, there was usually one short season of economic activity in the tropical monsoon region. The busiest season happened not in the rainiest months but early in the winter when the rain-fed crops came into the market. Wages and interest rates rose to high levels. The slack season was very slack. Wages and interest rates fell as labor was in surplus and capital idle. All agricultural societies experience seasonality. The tropical monsoon regions experienced extreme degrees of seasonality.

WHY CLIMATE MATTERS

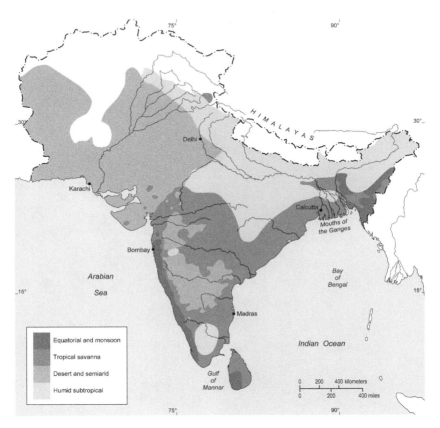

Figure 1.1 Climate of South Asia excluding Nepal (around 2015)

* * *

People living under tropical aridity and the monsoon tried to adapt to these conditions. How did they adapt? Reconstruction of climate history for South Asia based on pollen and tree-ring data suggests that the southwest monsoon strengthened in the mid- to late Holocene period. That process gradually turned a cool, dry savanna into a warm tropical and

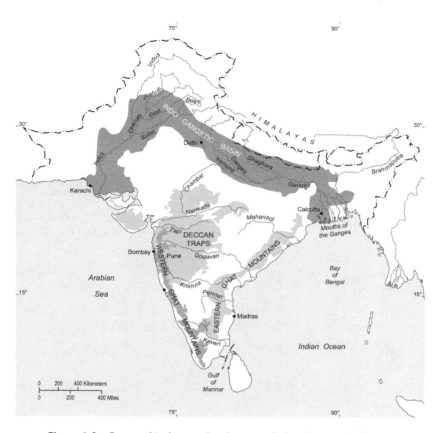

Figure 1.2 Geographical zones, South Asia excluding Nepal and Afghanistan (around 2015)

seasonally modulated climate about three to four thousand years ago.[9] Since then, adaptation to monsoon variability, or adapting to the risks of floods and droughts, has been crucial for the people who live in southern Asia.

What actions could those living in the countryside take to mitigate floods and famines? Migration and transhumance were a response to famines. These moves carried costs, and for most of the agricultural population whose only asset was a fixed plot of land, other mitigation strategies would be necessary. The most secure form of mitigation would be creating access to controllable and reliable sources of water. A reliable source is a rechargeable source where the user can harvest water throughout the year. A controllable source is where the user can control the volume of extraction, making intensive cultivation profitable. A deep well in a large aquifer is an example of a secure and controllable source, as opposed to seasonally variable sources such as streams and ponds, where evaporation occurs at a much faster rate.

No wonder, then, that water conservation in South Asia has an ancient history. Environmental historians have studied small and large water storage and distribution systems that were in use centuries, even millennia, before the present times and have drawn valuable inferences about the states and institutions that created and maintained these (figure 1.3). The scholarship offers one robust conclusion. No matter when or where we look, we will find states and communities that tried to store monsoon rainwater for use in the drier seasons. They also built dams to prevent floods. That these steps were necessary for survival was common knowledge to the communities.[10]

Environmental history recognizes that these responses existed. Economic historians, who seek the roots of economic growth and inequality in the deep past, would go further and ask how good they were and what they were good for. Management of water mattered crucially to both growth and inequality. Did communities succeed in turning water control into an instrument powerful enough to carry out intensive agriculture and sustain population growth? Floods and

Figure 1.3 Step well in western India. Several thousand step wells like these existed from the ancient times in the arid areas of India. Water occurred below ground at the same level as a normal well. The elaborate construction became an architectural statement as well as a cool resting place. Deep step wells reduced the evaporation rate considerably. Step wells were costly to build and maintain, vulnerable to a fall in the water table, and sometimes a health hazard. Most were abandoned. Pictured here is Chand Baori in eastern Rajasthan state, built between the eighth and sixteenth centuries. Credit: Carroll Apiez and Shutterstock.

famines exposed communities to the risk of mass death. When floods and famines happened, whose lives did the community save? For whom did water control work?

We can answer these questions by working backward from the more modern times. Statistical data on living standards across countries find that India was an impoverished region from long before the nineteenth century.[11] These comparisons often use doubtful benchmarks, such as wages paid to workers when few details are available on employment conditions. Even when allowance is made for that, there is no doubt that, on average, Indians were poor by world standards for a long time in the past.

There was, however, no such thing as an average Indian. Some of the wages available in the 1500s or 1600s came from the Mughal imperial cities or the seaboard, which did not face water shortages, offered year-round markets for labor, and wanted craft skills of various sorts. Wages were high in these settings, not much behind wages in London or Amsterdam. Observing these wages, economic historians sometimes wrongly conclude that Indians were lavishly well-off three hundred years ago. Most farm laborer wages would have been a fraction of these urban wages. A historian of Mughal India, W. H. Moreland, looked at some of the sources on standards of living and inclined toward the view of the Dutch merchant Francisco Pelsaert that the "common people" in India were "poor wretches" whose lives were little better than those of "contemptible earthworms."[12] We need not go as far as that, but it is indisputable that the poor in India were *poor* about three hundred years ago and that most people were poor.

This statistical scholarship does not explain why there was widespread poverty in the region. The most reasonable answer is low agricultural yield and unemployment of resources. If the idea of water recycling was well known, the practice fell far short of securing prosperous livelihoods. There were broadly two reasons why the practice fell short.

The first reason was property right. About 1850 in India, fixed pools like the step well in figure 1.3, were usually privately or communally owned. The most secure form of supply came from masonry wells. Wells, too, were usually privately owned. "The main opening for individual enterprise," the *Imperial Gazetteer* of 1909 noted, "lies in the construction of wells."[13] In southern India, artificial lakes, called tanks, provided a measure of security for rich and poor alike.[14] But tanks were expensive to build and maintain, tanks entailed inequality of rights of access, and successive dry seasons reduced most tanks' capacity.

The second reason was the limited scale of even the biggest irrigation works that were built. The monsoon rains made planting relatively easy in most parts of India. The usual practice in the nineteenth century was to have two plantings in the monsoon, of which one was a major grain. In some regions, a weak winter monsoon enabled a second and minor crop. Growing any of the major grains in winter or some profitable year-round crops such as sugarcane depended on irrigation that required either impounding rain and river flows or digging underground. If we exclude one or two large artificial lakes, collective effort was insufficient to achieve both forms of recycling on a large scale. Monsoon dependence, therefore, meant unemployment for months.

That is not all. Life expectancy would be low in an environment with high climatic risk or the risk of floods and famines. Almost all historical population figures for India are speculative and come with a wide margin of error. Most estimates form a range. Opposite results follow if a low estimate pairs with a high estimate from another time. Some patterns still stand out. The discussion on population trends before 1920 revolves around whether there was any increase at all and not on the scale of the increase. Among the more reasonable guesstimates, the population increased by 0.1–0.2 percent per year in 1700–1821, and the rate rose to 0.3–0.4 percent in the next one hundred years.[15] Numbers relating to the long run make little sense but do not suggest a significantly different growth rate in times past. After 1921, however, there was a sharp and irreversible upturn. The rate exceeded 1 percent and accelerated rapidly. Decadal censuses began in 1872. If the post-census regional variation indicates past patterns, then population growth in 1700–1921 would have been higher and steadier in the well-watered Indo-Gangetic basin and near zero and volatile in the rain-dependent semiarid peninsula (figure 1.2). That regional difference suggests that demographic transition in the driest regions needed water intervention on a large scale. Water did begin to make a difference from the early twentieth century on.

At the end of the nineteenth century, when demographic data improved in quality, the role of dryland famines in causing mass death was well known. Famines happened if two successive monsoons failed or the southwest monsoon and the northeast monsoon failed in the same year. Suffering, however, occurred in a graded way, depending on the level of access that groups had to the secure water sources. The norms and rules of society shaped that access. Famine reports from later times revealed that most deaths from exceptional droughts occurred among the "low caste" population. One reason was that some castes, because of their status, had a ritually weak entitlement to secure water sources. It would follow that a permanent fall in deaths from famines could take place because a deep-rooted pattern of social inequality became weaker.

In short, around the turn of the twentieth century, the trajectory of economic growth and inequality changed. A series of interventions that changed the quality of adaptation to monsoon variability made that possible. Water access is crucial to the story. If water was a constraint on population growth earlier, that constraint eased off. New irrigation works enlarged the scale of water recycling. Cities saw water storage and redistribution on an unprecedented scale. Over 130 years, per capita water use increased three times (table 1.1), population six times, and total water use more than twenty times, and food-grain production increased from 15–20 million tons in 1885 to 50 million tons in 1950 and more than 250 million tons in 2015. Except for 1920–1970, South Asia's average income grew at a similar or higher rate than the average world income. Water technology extraction, state intervention, and access laws all changed after India gained independence from British rule in 1947. But the trajectory was colonial in origin.

Water access is one part of the story. For capital and labor, accessing job opportunities for part of the year is another. In 1954, a government survey of rural labor found that most people in the countryside faced, on average, one hundred

Table 1.1 Water use, 1885–2015: Total and per head (annual)

	Agricultural use (bcm)	Consumption and industrial use (bcm)	Total water use (bcm)	Population (million, undivided India until 1938)	Per capita water use (cm)
1885	43	6	50	260	192
1938	125	9	134	380	352
1968	309	15	324	535	606
1988	460	40	500	830	602
2015	876	124	1,000	1,310	763

Sources: Tirthankar Roy, "Water, Climate, and Economy in India from 1880 to the Present," *Journal of Interdisciplinary History* 51, no. 4 (Spring 2021): 565–594.
Notes: bcm = billion cubic meters; cm = cubic meters.

days of enforced unemployment and partial unemployment almost throughout the year. Banking statistics from the 1880s showed that the harvest season interest rates were three times higher than the rates in the slack season. The only effective mitigation to such extreme degrees of seasonality was a reallocation of capital and labor between livelihoods and regions that faced seasonality on different scales. From the late 1800s on, workers and financiers did use these strategies more often. A great fall in transport and communications costs interlinked many labor markets, enabling some people trapped in season-bound livelihoods to combine other jobs in different places. Seasonal short-distance migration increased, and the financial market diversified.

Not all parts of southern Asia experienced the tropical monsoon in the same way. The Bengal delta and Kerala faced aridity at times but had a lot more surface water. The seaboard, too, was an exception to the norm. It had a milder climate and access to deltas and estuaries. In the time span of interest, port cities like Bombay, Calcutta, and Madras, the main commercial centers, were less susceptible to seasonality. With globalization and expansion of commodity export trade, the less water-stressed seaboard played a more significant role in driving economic change from the mid-nineteenth century on, attracting migrants from the rural inland. The migration put pressure on the quality of life in the cities, causing epidemic outbreaks. But the cities were free of famines. Thanks to many potential taxpayers, and some measure of self-governance, the municipalities could move to create large-scale waterworks. Outside the cities, making more water accessible to more people through the year was easier to achieve in the river valleys, the floodplains of the Himalayan rivers, and wetland zones in the east. These areas, too, experienced mitigation of water insecurity and seasonal unemployment. The achievement came at a cost. The cost gives sustainability of economic growth in monsoon economies a definite meaning.

* * *

Available water stock as a proportion of renewable sources fell (table 1.2). The World Bank measures water stress as the withdrawal of freshwater as a percentage of renewable supply. In 2016, levels of stress ranged from 42 percent in India to 105 percent in Pakistan. The levels were considerably lower in the UK (10), the US (22), Japan (28), and China (30).[16] There is a close across-country correlation between average temperature, latitude, and stress, suggesting that the stress pattern is geographical in origin. With a lot of renewable water remaining unused, the high use-to-stock ratio may

Table 1.2 Renewable water resource (cubic meters per head)

	India	UK	US	Japan	Exploitable water resource available (%)
1968	3,600	2,577	14,072	4,257	70
1988	2,280	2,591	11,938	3,495	54
2015	1,480	2,191	9,075	3,385	8

Source: Food and Agriculture Organization of the United Nations, AQUASTAT database, http://www.fao.org/nr/water/aquastat/data/query/results.html
Notes: Exploitable resource = total renewable resource (surface water + groundwater − overlap)—environmental flow requirement for the sustainability of the aquatic system. The figure for India is 1,089 bcm during the year (2015). I hold the number constant for all times. Usable resource is (1—use/resource).

not seem like a tragedy. But the marginal cost of using the resource is high in South Asia and rising.

How do we know that it is high? First, not all the available water should be exploited, and the proportion of still-unused to exploitable resource fell at a steeper rate in the late twentieth century. Second, the proportion of groundwater extraction seems to have increased (the data are not complete), and groundwater extraction is more expensive than surface water use. Already, the extraction of renewable sources generates higher costs (deeper bore wells) and poorer quality (brackish water, contaminated aquifers) than in the past. Third, hydropolitics has grown more disputatious as these changes have happened.

The narrative that I offer, therefore, resembles a cross. Access increased in the long run, whereas stress increased simultaneously, or usable water reserve fell sharply. Geography limited the "degrees of freedom" to sustain continually improving per capita entitlement. Most societies in the twentieth century would have experienced a cross. It is the steep slope of the stress curve in India that is unusual and worrying.

* * *

Is the book doing something that has been done before? In specific contexts, historians of India make a connection between the environment and the economy. When relevant, such works will be cited. However, as a generalization, the following statement may still hold. There is not yet a body of writings that uses Indian material and asks the question that I am trying to answer: how human activities working on the environment enabled economic growth and population transition. Historical scholarship either on the economy or on the environment is yet to note what I have called the water cross.

Early European writings on Asiatic societies, to which Karl Marx, Karl Wittfogel, and Fernand Braudel contributed, claimed that water control was a crucial matter in the world's drylands. Waterworks, in turn, involved public investment and top-down command systems and, therefore, needed despotic states. These writings contained neither serious research on the tropics nor reliable environmental histories. They were not meant to be either. They were theories of the Asiatic state, trying to confirm a hunch that the concept of private property was well developed in Europe and weak in Asia before industrialization. If the state was as powerful as claimed, the societies were vulnerable and changeless. Any real change came with European expansion in the eighteenth century, as Marx explained. The image of inertia carried over into present-day writings about Indian history, for example, into Eric Jones's "indestructible atoms" that composed India, the atoms being "village agriculture," and the "caste system."[17] Caste does matter to Indian history, but a realistic theory of why it mattered does not follow from these Europeanist accounts of Asia.

Comparative economic history has been unmindful and often unsophisticated about the role of geography in shaping human lives and the impact of human activities on their environment. Natural resource endowments do receive attention. But the geographical agency, when we include in that concept climate, soil, elevation, and vegetation, is a more extensive idea than resource extraction. Besides, resource endowment is a biased concept. The notion of what resources matter to economic change depends (for most economic historians) on what resources mattered for nineteenth-century Britain. The critical natural resource is fossil fuel. The book will claim that water was a more valuable economic resource for the tropical monsoon regions than energy and that water extraction had a more profound impact on local environments than the burning of fuels. The meaning of Anthropocene in popular discourse is yet to take complete account of this difference.

There is, moreover, a methodological problem at the heart of comparative economic history. Most economists like to measure desired economic change by average or per capita income, a ratio of income and population. Income appears as the numerator and population as the denominator. Raising life span was a more significant challenge in tropical societies than in temperate ones. If a tropical region succeeded in meeting the challenge, its average income growth would be low, and economists would call that phenomenon—perversely—a failure. In India, the average income trend was relatively flat for a long time because a revolution had begun in water distribution, which raised life spans and had a modest impact on incomes.

Global environmental history, by and large, has overlooked the implications of the tropical monsoon condition for economic change. *The Oxford Handbook of Environmental History* does not mention the word *monsoon*.[18] An ambitious study of the world's arid regions questions many Europeanist preconceptions about tropical lands but does not engage with the combination of aridity and the monsoon that produces seasonality, which defines South Asia's situation.[19] A recent book suggests that, in South Asian history, control of rivers secured livelihoods. Unlike the author of that book, I am interested in explaining the modern economic history of the region.[20] The Indianist environmental history is a rich scholarship.[21] And a part of it is about water.[22] Insightful on imperialism, and mainly about imperialism, the scholarship does not ask questions that economic historians ask. It is of little use in understanding the roots of economic growth, population growth, and inequality.

Development economics in the postwar years was interested in geography but rarely discussed water. In the 1980s, an offshoot of the field coined the phrase "monsoon Asia" to show why some monsoon regions facing seasonal unemployment needed to prioritize labor-absorbing activities.[23] Rather like the Europe-centered Asian history, these works were aiming to explain the economic rise of Japan. The Japan-centric concept of monsoon Asia did not deal with aridity. Therefore, it did not apply well to the tropical monsoon areas. By underestimating aridity, the idea of monsoon Asia imposed an artificial uniformity over a diverse geographical area.

A major theme in the book is "stress," or the risk of a fall in quantity and quality of water with increased use. The sustainability of an economic-cum-demographic trajectory that water had made possible is of vital importance. However, the literature on sustainability is of limited use in the present case because it overlooks the specific conditions of monsoon economies. The formative writings by Garrett Hardin and Elinor Ostrom turned the attention of scholars to the common property resource problem. As understood in ecology and economic theory, the tragedy of the commons occurs when many people exploit a common property resource, leading to its loss. The implication is that some old rules of exploitation that could provide good results, what Hardin called "social arrangements that produce responsibility," were given up in the process and that new cooperative rules needed designing.[24] The "tragedy" perspective spawned important works on water, which I cite in specific contexts. The resource problem discussed in the book is not an overuse problem, however. Instead, it stems from an initial condition that climate and geology had created. That condition entailed deprivation and threat. The commons came under pressure because of a welfare-raising response to deprivation and threat, hardly a tragedy.

If climate and water do enter comparative analysis sometimes, comparative history almost totally overlooks seasonality. Seasonality, of course, exists in all agricultural societies. The degree of it differs. A rough measure of seasonality is monthly interest rate fluctuations. The economist Simon Kuznets estimated an index for the pre-depression US.[25] The busy season interest rate was 2–5 percent of the slack season in his data set. It was 250–300 percent in India. Both countries had similar banks and similar laws about banking. Their difference stemmed from the climate. The difference was more than a matter of degree. It left the latter region with a long idle season and a lot fewer investment opportunities.

* * *

To sum up, the book makes five connected points.

First, the tropical monsoon climate makes economic and population growth contingent on water security. In the nineteenth century, poverty and famines in the drylands of India were manifestations of water insecurity. Second, steps to achieve security enabled intensive agriculture, urbanization, and mortality decline in the region. Third, in a water-scarce world, the means adopted to deal with the insecurity impaired sustainability and raised stress. Fourth, just as new measures to deal with water access emerged since the nineteenth century, similarly (and in part because of these measures), a set of actions emerged that increased labor and capital mobility between working seasons. These actions, too, came with costs. Fifth, the story has lessons about how we should write the economic history of a world facing environmental degradation of different kinds.

I develop the narrative over six chapters. Having suggested that a set of human actions mitigated the climatic constraint on demographic and economic change since 1880, in the rest of the book I investigate what these actions were, why they appeared in the late nineteenth century, and what the costs were. I show that famine relief policy in the late nineteenth century, which defined the "water famine" as a seasonal condition, introduced the concept of the public trust in water (chapter 2). Chapter 3 looks at political movements that attacked the socially sanctioned forms of deprivation. Chapter 4 considers public intervention; chapter 5, the cities; and chapter 6, water stress. Chapter 7 deals with seasonality. The last chapter, chapter 8, called "Monsoon Economies," explores the implications of Indian history for comparative history.

2

WATER AND FAMINE

The famine was a famine of water . . .
—Indian Famine Commission, 1899

In 1877, a British journalist moved to India to take over as the editor of the *Madras Times*. His first task was to cover the famine then raging in the districts about two hundred miles to the west of Madras town. He toured, wrote down what he saw, and campaigned for public charity. What he saw was not just hunger, something charity might help with. He saw a desperate search for moisture everywhere, something no charity or public funds could solve. Grim villagers "excavated . . . failing wells deeper and deeper in the rocky strata." They "delved for springs and under-currents of water in the sandy beds of the dry river."[1] They dropped a bucket in a nearly dry well at nightfall, hoping the morning would see a little muddy liquid accumulate in it. He saw "universal drying-up of the tanks," or artificial lakes, on a scale that had "hardly been witnessed within the memory of living man."[2] William Digby followed his famine report with a scathing book arguing that India's poverty and famine resulted from the failure of British colonial rule (1857–1947), among other ways, to provide water when the rains failed.[3] In a different way, an official commission of inquiry delivered the same conclusion.

In the next twenty years, two more famines broke out in the Deccan, the plateau that forms the central part of the peninsular region in South Asia. The epicenter of the 1876–1877 famine was in the southern districts, then called the Madras-Deccan and now the southwestern part of the Andhra Pradesh state of India. The other two famines, in 1896–1897 and 1898–1899, occurred on the northwestern side of the plateau, or the area then known as the Bombay-Deccan.

Famines of devastating impact like the three had happened before in southern Asia. These famines were a break from the past because they produced a large volume of documentation, feeding into a search for a theory of dryland famines. The theory that emerged said that famines were a feature of the tropical monsoon climate and could be prevented with an adequate expansion of canal irrigation to increase food production and a railway to transport food faster when the monsoon failed. What followed the plan is something of a puzzle.

Famines disappeared from the Deccan after 1900. Weather shocks of almost similar severity repeated in 1900–1947 in at least four years. "Yet the potential dangers were largely dealt with."[4] What had happened to make that possible? Economic historians suggest that some aspects of the famine mitigation policy—especially the development of the railways as food carriers—did contain the damaging effects of the droughts (see below). The account is incomplete because it ignores water. Famine documents made a distinction between a famine of food and one of water. Railways could potentially solve the famine of food. They could not lessen a famine of water.

As for irrigation as a preventive measure, elements of the plan did materialize in the wetter deltas and the Indo-Gangetic basin. There was little breakthrough in the drier Deccan. And yet, famines did disappear in the Deccan after 1900.

Historians of famine have missed an important message the reports delivered. The reports reveal a growing local awareness that the solution to the Deccan water problem demanded a different model from the riparian one the official policy endorsed. It required reliance on *subsoil* water, access to which was restricted by property law and by caste status. Insurance against famine meant the security of a well, an expensive form of asset. The famine relief, therefore, led to the construction of wells and sometimes sequestration of wells.[5] The water-specific actions contributed to no small extent to the disappearance of famines. At the very least, these steps introduced the concept of the public trust in underground resources, a radical idea for the time.

What was it about the Deccan that made water so difficult an issue to resolve?

* * *

The Deccan received far smaller monsoon rainfall than the coasts and the deltas (figure 2.1). The years of the three Deccan famines saw unusual climatic conditions caused by the El Niño Southern Oscillation phenomenon. The year 1877 was the driest in over a century (1871–1978) for which rainfall data exist. The average rainfall in that year was 30 percent short of the long-term level. A 25 percent shortfall developed again in 1896 and 1899, and also in 1918. Only one more drought year in Indian history, 1972, saw a rainfall deficit of similar magnitude.[6] On the four earlier occasions, mass deaths followed. Although more people died of the influenza pandemic than a famine in 1918, an indirect link between drought and disease was likely. Compared with the recent past, famine deaths dropped from 1900. Rain deficits of slightly smaller magnitude than 30 percent had caused famines over smaller areas in earlier times. Deficits of such order did not cause famines anymore after 1900.

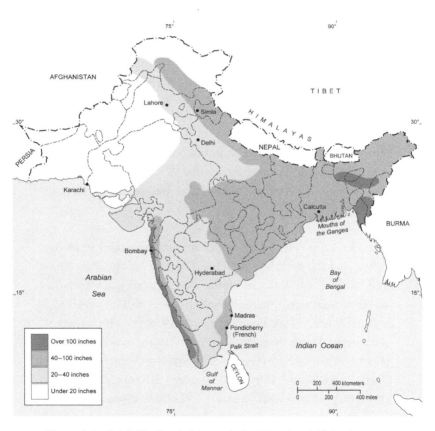

Figure 2.1 Rainfall in South Asia, excluding Nepal and Afghanistan

Monsoon failure was devastating in the Deccan because of its geology. The larger part of the plateau in its northwestern side, the so-called Deccan Traps, was formed of late Mesozoic volcanic eruptions (sixty to sixty-five million years ago). The southern and eastern sides of the Deccan uplands formed parts of the Gondwana continent that drifted away from Africa and collided with the Eurasian plate about forty to fifty-five million years ago, creating the Himalayan mountains. Because of their different geological origins, the soil and rock types vary between these zones. Both regions, however, have hard rock formations. The pattern of precipitation also imparts uniformity to both areas. The rain-bearing clouds of the southwest monsoon lose a lot of their moisture when crossing the Western Ghat mountains. The hotter air of the plateau creates a convectional process that produces storms and causes the air to cool. Still, seasonal rainfall reduces to less than a third of that on the windward side of the mountains.

Although the Deccan received smaller quantities of annual monsoon rainfall than eastern or coastal India, it was not the driest part of India. Besides, as the mountain range has few gaps along its north-south expanse for a thousand miles, a lot of the rainwater flows down the eastern slope into the plateau and forms the so-called Ghat-fed rivers. The Godavari and the Krishna, and the two tributaries of Krishna, the Bhima and the Tungabhadra, carry most of the monsoon flow (figure 1.2). Between them, the Godavari and the Krishna drainage areas cover more than two-thirds of the plateau. Still, "the Deccan rivers cannot be depended upon as a perennial source of supply."[7] Whereas in northern India the rivers received snowmelt, the Deccan rivers did not, and, therefore, the flow level varied enormously between seasons. On an October day in 1903, more than a million cubic feet per second (cusecs) flowed near Vijayawada town, about seventy miles inland from the mouth of the Krishna River. In the summer months around that time, the level fell to a few hundred cusecs. During the dry season of 1899, the mighty Krishna and Godavari were "reduced to a series of shallow pools."[8] For eight months in a year, the rivers did not carry much water to sustain intensive agriculture or a large population.

Except in the deltas, cultivation and survival were dependent on tanks and wells instead of the rivers. Wells were not easy to build. The aquifers in the Deccan Traps occur in fissures in between layers of hard rocks. Some of these fissures are formed of successive volcanic eruptions. In the alluvial Gangetic basin, subsoil water can be found almost everywhere. In the Deccan Traps, the occurrence of subsoil water depends on the position of a fissure. Having to dig through basaltic rock made the construction of a well an expensive proposition and a risky one as well. "There is by no means a certainty of meeting water. The Deccan . . . is full of wells which have been dug and been failures. . . . [T]he percentage of failures among wells [cannot] be less than forty per cent."[9] Even when the effort was successful, successive dry seasons could reduce water in wells to dangerously low levels.

Local chiefs and warlords devoted money and power to the construction of tanks (lakes), using forced labor in the process. These tanks dotted the Tamil Nadu countryside and a large area in southern Karnataka, or the former Mysore state. Most survive today. The tanks came in a wide range of sizes and capacities. With a few exceptions, the best of them provided a slightly higher level of water security to the population than rivers did. When the rains failed, most smaller tanks dried up, as during the 1896–1897 famine in Bombay. Geodetic Satellite or GeoSat images taken around 2001 confirmed that tanks were rarely used for irrigation, even in recent times, because "by the end of the dry season the tanks have shrunk to a fraction of their normal size."[10] The right to tank water was more democratic than the right to well water, but there is no evidence to suggest that the neediest had access to the water in a famine. During severe droughts, when the subsoil water level fell, the tank became a disease carrier. The conducting of "personal ablutions, washing of clothes and utensils, and watering of cattle" in the same place turned it into a "source of pestilence."[11]

In the Bombay and Madras regions, the main monsoon crops were millets and rice in the lowlands that trapped more water. There was usually a winter crop, rice planted in December and cut in May, only in the coastal and deltaic regions where a winter monsoon occurred or when either river or tank water was available. Such intensive agricultural regimes were more common in the deltas of the Godavari, Krishna, and Kaveri. Except in the deltas and in proximity to the larger tanks, cultivation was rain-dependent. The drinking water throughout the region came from storages such as wells and tanks.

The value of the wells had become common knowledge in famine operations since the 1876–1878 episode. Still, the civil administration in most provinces did not collect or record data on the quantity and depth of subsoil water. The famines underscored how weak the water statistics were so far. "A great deal has been written about water-supply and subsoil water [in Gujarat], as also on the possibility of tapping artisan [*sic*] wells, but so far as my knowledge goes there is little or no reliable data to go upon," an officer reported.[12] With the 1876 disaster fresh in memory, officers were looking for data on subsoil water to gauge the scale of the problem when a period of dryness hit the trap area of the western Deccan in 1896.

There was a way to get the statistics.

* * *

Trains running along the Great Indian Peninsula Railway's line connecting Bombay with Madras obtained water for the locomotives from wells along the way. For internal recordkeeping, the train guards wrote down the condition of these wells in a logbook. At the onset of the 1898 famine, local officers sought the railway data. The company gave them levels of water in the same set of wells recorded for ten years. The numbers told a shocking story. A period of relative dryness had caused an almost "total disappearance of a huge volume of subterranean water all over the Deccan, on which it was formerly possible to draw in a year of drought."[13]

Soon, more specific reports started coming in from other regions, with the same message. "The level of the sub-soil water has never been so low within living memory . . . [in all] districts of the Deccan and Karnatak."[14] In the Sholapur District, tanks still had some water in them, but the level had gone down so much that what remained was preserved for drinking, and there was none for cultivation. "In many places, do what one may, no water is to be got."[15] The same story repeated in many small towns in the Bombay-Deccan and the army bases. "The rain we have just had has been all absorbed by the parched surface soil and has not replenished the spring."[16]

Local officers understood that subsoil water was the crucial warning sign, though the administration did not back up their hunch with a monitoring system.[17] Between 1876 and 1899, the administrative correspondence applied the phrase "water

WATER AND FAMINE

famine" often.[18] The words filtered into the growing media discourse on famines. "You may see whole villages deserted," the *Times of India* wrote in 1900, "because of the exhaustion of the water supply," and called the calamity a water famine.[19] The prospect of a water famine was "alarming" because it unleashed epidemics. Water shortage made it difficult to use bullocks to transport grain and to lift water from deep wells.

Importing food from outside the region could end a famine of food, but it was no solution to a water famine (see, however, figure 2.2). "The shortage of drinking water

Figure 2.2 Women and children collect water brought by train (June 2000). There is no record of mass transportation of water in the nineteenth century. But trains did transport water during more recent droughts. Women and girls would usually fetch water for the family, spending an enormous amount of time to do so. The picture shows that sometimes they took great risks. The train carrying water during a three-year drought has stopped at Luni Junction near Jodhpur, western India. The water it is carrying is not meant for those who are filling pitchers. Credit: Roger Lemoyne and Getty Images.

is . . . naturally more dreaded than a failure of food crops and is also more difficult to be combated."[20] Railways were no answer to diseases either. Famine historians observe that cholera was a thorough killer in a famine year, accounting for about a quarter of all deaths.[21] Administrators understood the connection. "Famine and pestilence," stated the 1880 Famine Commission report, "are the twin-offspring of the drought."[22] Cholera was a waterborne disease. Cholera was also a killer; left untreated, death from cholera rose to 50–80 percent. Those who survived that risk still suffered greatly from the less fatal but debilitating enteric diseases. "The scanty water-supply is at the bottom of the trouble."[23]

State relief was often too little and came too late. Yet, it introduced two principles about groundwater that were new to the region. Wells were a private asset, not only in the Deccan but everywhere. If wells were the last resort, the authorities would need to requisition private wells and improve the quality of well water. In an uncoordinated way, the relief effort involved both and created more of the only form of asset to mitigate drought and disease in the Deccan.

The relief camps were few and far between. A camp required a source of pure water supply. Otherwise, the concentration of many people in one place would turn the camp into a breeding ground for cholera. Even when water was available near a camp, a difficult condition to meet, "individual works [had] to be small as to numbers owing to a short supply of water."[24] Following the English workhouse tradition, the people who came to the relief camps were required to supply labor for food if they were physically able to work. In water-rich areas where the famine was a famine of food, the camps gave work and food if the workers brought their water for the day.[25] That option did not exist in the Deccan. The first task, therefore, was to dig a well. There was no certainty that a new well would produce enough water. It was dangerous to have that effort fail. When the attempt did fail, the relief seekers turned to the stagnant pools of polluted water found on the beds of rivers nearby. "Strenuous efforts are made," frustrated officers wrote, "to prevent relief workers at camps from taking water from these vitiated sources; but . . . it is difficult to enforce this even at the camps."[26] The death rate from cholera, therefore, was much higher in the countryside.

Despite reverses, the campaign succeeded. Cholera was contained. By disinfecting wells, taking over some, and building new ones, the relief system could widen access to clean water. "The disease," the report on the 1899–1900 famine in central India observed, "has almost everywhere been successfully stamped out on the works themselves, but with the bad water supply it was impossible to eradicate it from the villages."[27]

The officers thus observed a connection between drought, groundwater, property right, and cholera. There was a fifth and awkward element in the combination—religion. Owners of wells did not welcome the interference from engineers and famine officers and resented having to share the water. Their reason for doing so was couched in the language of caste. Sharing water with the lower castes was a religious taboo for the upper-caste people. The camps were already dealing with segregation of kitchens and dwelling places by caste and could do little to counter the sentiment. Some relief officers would share that sentiment. When a private well was requisitioned, the officers had to hire only upper-caste individuals to carry water.[28] Segregation was a poor strategy, but still a strategy. Where possible, "low caste people were . . . given separate wells."[29] The Bombay Famine Code directed the medical officers on duty "to watch the state of the water-supply . . . allotted to the low-caste people."[30]

Caste and cholera were so interdependent that the famine authorities could not save lives without interference in caste matters. "The risk of interfering with prejudice," the 1880 Famine Commission observed with regret, "frequently stand[s] in the way of improvement."[31] When the famine was at its most intense, social inequality became even more insidious than normal. Richard Temple, governor of Bombay, observed during the 1876–1877 famine that the "humble castes and classes of field laborers, . . . rude artisans and . . . village menials" were the greatest sufferers from the calamity.[32] They suffered because in few villages did the lower castes have the right to use the communal well during droughts. During the 1899 famine, again, local officers found that "as to the 'caste' of those died, by far the great majority [were] 'Hindus of low caste.'"[33] Members of the depressed castes relied on the contaminated ponds, whereas the village elite guarded the wells.[34]

In 1898 and 1899, the officers were more active than they had been twenty years earlier. They were more ready to requisition a private well, using administrative powers to override the legally secure private rights.[35] Although the British Indian state was reluctant to revoke caste privileges, during the 1899 famine the relief authorities often did just that. A great many wells came up with the relief money.

The authorities wanted access to private or community wells also to increase their capacity. During 1896–1897, famine relief included a policy "to deepen wells when necessary and advisable; and to sink new wells in districts where they may be necessary to prevent migration of cattle and people."[36]

The call to deepen wells was a constant refrain in the western Deccan as a way to avoid the prospect of a water famine.

The concern with water in this way changed from quantity to safety between 1876 and 1900, a shift that deserves emphasis, seeing how profoundly famine historians missed noticing it.[37]

* * *

Comparing the 1880 Famine Commission report with its counterpart in 1901, we can find a shift in the official famine analysts' view on why water control was necessary for famine prevention. In 1880, water was required to raise food production. Food, and the railways to deliver food faster, was the critical element of a famine policy. By 1901, the accent had shifted to disease. The change of mind came from the knowledge that cholera took more lives than starvation and that not only secure but also *safe* water was a private good.[38]

Cholera was a disease indigenous to India. Its original home was the middle Bengal delta. However, from a major outbreak in 1817 onward, the disease spread outward, reaching Europe, North America, Russia, Southeast Asia, and the Middle East by the second quarter of the nineteenth century. Ships, migrants, and hajj pilgrims took it far afield. These channels of transmission are well known. Rather less known are the channels that spread the disease inside India. The Deccan plateau region was not the natural home of the disease, nor was there known population exchange between the middle Bengal countryside and the Deccan. The first outbreaks, therefore, remain a mystery. Once cholera appeared there, it spread like a forest fire. By 1876, the association of cholera with water was established thanks to research done in London in the 1850s. By 1896, the bacillus that caused the disease had been identified, by the German bacteriologist Robert Koch, who did a part of his research in India. The research showed that the bacillus lived in water. A vaccine was still far away, and the hope of mass inoculation a dream. Doctors and officers on the ground had to do something about water quality.

Around 1860, a sanitary commission investigated the conditions of health in the Indian army. Shortly after its report revealed appalling hygiene conditions in the barracks, a sanitary commissioner's office appeared in the Bombay and Madras Provinces. The water quality of the military camps was an immediate target. Outside such precise sites, the commissioner's duties were confined to information gathering. It was a department of minor importance. The provincial governments had too little funds to shore up the work.

Cholera defined the purpose of the sanitation staff more sharply and placed them at the center of famine operations. The department disinfected wells on an extensive scale and fought with the owners of wells who did not want such interference. The appointment of sanitary engineers took these activities to a new level. The engineers' first task was to conduct surveys to prevent epidemics. The reports focused on an action point: reduce contamination of drinking water. With the Public Works Department joining the project, "a large volume of work on several water-supply and drainage schemes was turned out in the nineties."[39] It was not smooth sailing. In Madras, for example, the sanitary engineer moved between autonomy and the authority of the Public Works Department. Still, the water-cleaning campaign delivered. Deaths from cholera fell from four per one thousand persons during its 1900 peak to less than one during the last big epidemic of 1935.

The intervention was chaotic. But lessons were learned.

* * *

One lesson was the need for data. The growing volume of famine reporting suggests a sense of purpose. The bulk of printed correspondence on the 1770 Bengal famine, the first major disaster the British colonial rulers of India had to deal with, would not exceed a hundred pages. The 1896–1897 Deccan famine produced published correspondence amounting to more than five thousand pages, not counting the private works written on the events. The documentation and analyses created a continuous memory of famines: from 1770 in Bengal to 1783 in northern India, 1833 in Guntur, 1837 in eastern India, Orissa in 1866, and the Deccan famines of 1876, 1896, and 1899. The later reports joined all past events together, drawing lessons about what had gone wrong in each case and what could have been done to save lives.

This documentation had no precedence in Indian history. Whereas the government data-collection system studied the post-1770 famines, knowledge of almost all pre-1770 episodes came from hagiographies of rulers (such as Ziauddin Barni's account of fourteenth-century North India), travelogues, and manuals on statecraft written by Brahmin priests. The two types of sources are not comparable. Hagiographies were few and far between, leading some famine historians to suggest (absurdly) that famines in the earlier times were few and far between. If the report of a past famine came from a hagiographic work, it would tell us that the king and the landlords looked after their people. Brahmin manuals almost always reminded the king of their sacred duty to feed the Brahmin when food ran short. None of these pre-British materials are reliable reflections of what happened when a famine broke out.[40] The British Indian reports, by contrast, were fact-finding inquiries, efforts of teams whose members did not always share the same interest and, therefore, could not push a single political line.

The knowledge delivered a better understanding of drought risk. By 1880, that understanding had hardened into an activist stance. India needed more artificial irrigation to make sure that food production was not too sensitive to rainfall. The reports of the Indian Famine Commission (1880, 1898, and 1901 and the Famine Enquiry Commission report of 1945), the report of the Indian Irrigation Commission (1901–1908), and the Famine Codes (1880 and provincial codes to follow) said that famines happened because of a risky agrarian environment. In a tropical region, water was a scarcer resource than land. When monsoon rain was the primary source of water, a significant risk was attached to water supply. Not all regions were affected equally. But those "poor in soil, their rain-fall precarious, [with] little . . . artificial irrigation [were] severely affected whenever drought visited."[41] In the late 1800s, administrators advocated irrigation works and restoration of disused tanks as insurance against future famines.

This accent on irrigation made a huge difference to the Indo-Gangetic basin and in the deltas, where topography and river structure made perennial canals possible. The basin was a flatland composed of alluvial sediments from the snowmelt rivers that descended from the Himalayas. These large perennial rivers carry more sediment than the monsoon-fed South Indian rivers, though alluvial flatlands do occur in the deltas of the monsoon rivers. Soil types vary within the basin. By and large, the soil here was porous and nutrient-rich (except for nitrogen content), the rivers in principle permitted canal irrigation, the alluvial land allowed well construction cheaply, and the combination of these factors sustained intensive agriculture. The basin and the deltas were already water-rich areas. The impact of the nineteenth-century famines was already milder here than in the dry south.

In South India, these conditions did not exist. Canals were no solution to the famines. Here, access to the groundwater was crucial, and that access bogged down in private rights to property and status. Water access was technologically challenging. More than that, it was legally challenging. It required administrative intervention and, as chapter 3 will show, a battle for equality of access. The famine documents showed a growing awareness of the problem.

Transport was the second main area of focus in 1880. Economic history scholarship acknowledges that the disappearance of dryland famines after 1900 was owed to an increase in railway density. First proposed by the historian Michelle B. McAlpin, the decisive role of the railways in the disappearance of famines from the Deccan plateau found confirmation in recent studies.[42] Contemporary administrators saw the connection. "The heaviest death-rate," wrote a report on the 1899–1900 episode, "occurred in those districts to which there was no direct access by railway or water."[43] Most railways were not built for famine relief. However, the lesson that private trade must be sustained during famines made it a handy weapon. Where there were no railways, the government committed to supplying other forms of transport to "encourage and stimulate trade."[44] Sustaining animal life was a necessary measure to reactivate local trade and return to cultivation.

But transport was no solution to water. The citation at the head of the chapter reflects a new awareness that the Deccan famines needed a distinct strategy. Railways would not be a part of that strategy, nor would canals. Wells were to be the center of the strategy. The aim was to increase access to subsoil water and make it safer to drink. Increasing reference to cholera and the more infrequent reference to irrigation and railways in the commission reports reflects a change of mind. During the famines of the Deccan uplands, the hundreds of thousands who died from cholera died not because they had grown weak but because they had to live on contaminated water when safe water sources dried up or the wealthy and upper-caste villagers guarded them.

Would the government have the means to supply clean water? Not necessarily, because most water bodies in the Deccan were underground, and the state had no lawful access to these wells. In 1876–1878, the local officers sat inert, not knowing how to proceed, but with a hunch that they needed to take over properties or build new ones to prevent deaths. That was a challenging task in a region with deep-rooted inequality, ruled by a state that swore by the sanctity of private property. Despite such a stance, many new wells were built in the trap area in the second and third famines. Many private and communal wells were requisitioned and cleaned. Doing so signified much more than famine relief. It was an assertion of the public trust doctrine to subsoil water, an assertion not backed up by a political commitment, but an assertion nonetheless.

* * *

Influenced by Edward Said's breathtaking claim that "neither imperialism nor colonialism is a simple act of accumulation and acquisition," that "both are supported and . . . impelled by . . . forms of knowledge affiliated with domination," postcolonial historians of Asia and Africa maintain that the scientific knowledge the imperial regimes gained about their colonies made them stronger than before.[45] These historians are wrong. What Europeans thought they knew about India took a huge hit every time a famine happened. The Deccan famines became an embarrassment for the empire. They exposed how little the administrators understood the geography and the people. Inequality among the affected populations was deep, and social practices allowed some members to die more readily than others. Controlling famine would involve knowing how to override that inequality. The officers of the state did not know how.

The state's knowledge was a work in progress. These moments of vulnerability for colonial science drove efforts to gather information and statistics, make inquiries and surveys, discard old theories, discover a new theory of origin, and design an action plan. That knowledge had a purpose. The purpose was not domination. It was saving lives. And it delivered just that. Deaths from cholera fell after 1900. Neither vaccines nor pretreated piped water alone could do the job. The famine reports showed why sanitation, food supply, and water access needed to combine in a relief-cum-prevention policy.

A series of catastrophic famines thus created an ecological discourse about economic change. The core idea was that the tropical monsoon climate elevated risks of droughts. The first action plan that followed the paradigm, one that stressed railways and canals as solutions, did not work well during the Deccan famines because canals were not a sustainable option in that geography, and cholera killed many people living on dwindling surface sources. Subsoil water was the key resource. The relief works in the 1890s ended up producing a lot more wells than before. When it started, the sanitation office lacked money, power, and purpose. The famine defined the role of the office. The efforts of the sanitation department made cholera less deadly than before.

All that effort saved lives and prevented deaths. It did not, however, improve agricultural conditions much. The beneficiaries of famine relief were too poor to possess enough land and access enough credit. Access to well water ensured their survival, but it was hardly a capital resource. Caste was a reason for their being so deprived. It was not as if the upper castes escaped unhurt. But the sufferings of the lower castes were greater. Mortality in the dryland famine was caste-biased because access to safe water was caste-biased. Colonialism, trapped in an ideology of noninterference in cultural matters, was an unlikely agent to break the norm. Within a few years after the last of the great dryland famines, a movement would form to challenge these biases.

3

WATER AND EQUALITY

As to the "caste" of those died [in 1899–1900], by far the great majority are "Hindus of low caste."
—Indian Famine Commission, 1902

The Untouchable does not want water. What he wants is *the right* to draw water from a common well.
—B. R. Ambedkar, 1932

These two quotations, thirty years apart, bookend a story. The distribution of water was status-based. And whereas distribution improved, the association of water access with status did not disappear. The famine relief operations changed distribution to some extent. Yet, the status-based right was embedded in practices and beliefs that the state could not reach and did not want to touch. The relief operation alone could not weaken the force of custom. Famine documents did, however, expose how deadly tradition had been during natural disasters. That knowledge was public when a struggle to wrest "the right to draw water from a common well" emerged early in the interwar years. Western India, where the memory of the famines was still fresh, was the stage. Chapter 3 describes that struggle.

A famine report of 1880 was the first systematic and large-scale demonstration of a connection between status and water access. Documents prepared during the two subsequent dryland famines to hit southern India made that connection more explicit. In a caste-divided community, access to the village well came with exclusions. Not only in the dry Deccan plateau, even in the water-rich Indo-Gangetic basin, the right to build and own a well was a privilege of status.[1]

Access to water, therefore, was segregated and unequal between families and communities. The private rights to secure supplies were guarded in the name of ritual purity. Famine mortality had a pronounced caste bias as a result. A relief officer may, in theory, sequester a well, but doing so amounted to an insult to religion. Officers did it more often than before (chapter 2). But a few officers could not overturn religion, nor did they want to. Anti-caste movements in the western Deccan learned the lesson and took the fight to the legislature and the court.

By the early 1900s, uncoordinated movements broke out in western India, involving an attempt to wrest control over wells and tanks from upper castes who had appropriated the right to these resources. In the interwar period, law and organized politics took over the campaign for equality of water rights in all parts of dry southern India. The jurist, politician, and social reformer B. R. Ambedkar's extensive writings and documentation of denial of civic rights to the people he termed the depressed castes revealed a growing number of instances when they asserted that right, especially in western and southern India, and faced resistance or violence. Chapter 3 tells how traditional privileges came under attack and generated a backlash in turn.

To talk about equality in an Indian setting means to talk about caste. I start by talking about caste.

* * *

In common uses of the phrase, the "caste system" could mean many things. One of these things was untouchability, an idea that emerged from a link between being a Brahmin and ritual purity or sacredness. The water rules derive from untouchability, not the caste system in a general sense.

Contemporary commentators on the movement treated these ideas as the legacy of an ancient set of entitlements. In 1936, as the leading spokesperson for the depressed castes, Ambedkar explained that legacy. The "annihilation of caste" was hard to achieve without radical methods because caste and sacredness were interdependent concepts.[2] The link between caste and sacredness implied a norm that sharing water with others caused pollution and loss of caste.

Interpretations of scriptures suggest that the moral rule was an inheritance from Indian tradition. Summing up a millennium of injunctions about caste, P. V. Kane said that "in most of the works on the castes in India a few features are pointed out as the characteristics of the caste system." One of these is who could (or could not) take water from whom.[3] The underlying idea was that water was not a shareable good, and rights were arranged by caste.[4] Classical Hindu writings on statecraft and social conduct are emphatic on the point.

A series of state-sponsored studies on "tribes and castes" around 1900 dealt with the caste-water link. Status is a relative thing. The authors of these reports sometimes struggled with finding an independent benchmark, a *numéraire*, with which they could create a tableau of status independent of subjective rankings. Some of them thought they found it in water rules. They defined status according to whom the Brahmins would share water with.[5] An imperial officer of Bengal, Herbert Hope Risley (1851–1911), produced a four-volume study of the tribes and castes of Bengal, which went further than the others in fixing status with reference to who would take water from whom. Risley's view carried weight. He was treated by many as an architect of ethnography and anthropometric research in India.

These attempts to find a practical rule by which those excluded from water access could be named, and their numbers measured, led to the invention of a series of terms—from *untouchable* drawn from texts to *depressed class* and *excluded caste*. In the twentieth century, nationalist and anti-caste political movements invented more names, *harijan*, *dalit*, and the official term *scheduled caste*. Why so many names? *Untouchable* stood for a ritually sanctioned practice. Almost all the other words stood for a rejection of that practice, in effect rejecting the ritualistic Hinduism that sanctioned exploitation.

This idea of an ancient legacy swayed some latter-day anthropologists. Louis Dumont's proposal that India was one civilization based on "a single true principle, namely the opposition of the pure and the impure," confirmed what the classical scholars had said about the origin of the rights to water.[6] The nature of that right was not proprietary in the modern sense. It was a moral right with a two-sided claim.[7] The Brahmin had a right to use a village well, and the untouchable had a religious duty *not* to use the same well. The two-sided right would appear to many people, including many untouchables and government officers, to keep the faith. Ambedkar's declaration—"The Untouchable does not want water. What he wants is *the right* to draw water from a common well"—points to the two-sided moral command.[8]

Colonial legal reforms may have played an indirect role in making the moral code more enforceable. In the nineteenth century, colonial property rights reform privileged ownership over user rights. That would mean that any well situated in a homestead land was private property, no matter that the water it drew on was common property. If status had an association with landholding or quality of dwelling, as it did, status also had an association with secure property in water because the homestead well was private property. Such a situation would give the upper castes control over water sanctioned in law *and* by religion.

Not all wells were in homestead land. Poorer villagers often drew water from one or two common wells. During famines and even in normal times, there were instances when the depressed castes lost access to the village well or tank or pond. Such exclusion had little to do with formal law. It had a lot to do with moral law. The moral right had such force that the famine relief authority needed to pussyfoot around such acts of capture. These instances suggest that the two-sided right to water appeared to many people as just.

Was that notion of justice old or new? Was it a part of Indian tradition? Or was it a colonial invention of tradition?

* * *

If Ambedkar and Dumont tell us that the inequality of rights to water inhered in Indian tradition, historians and anthropologists of more recent vintage tell us the opposite. By and large, the historiography of access to natural resources in India tends to be preoccupied with legal property rights rather than cultural norms. It also neglects water and water rights. Nevertheless, a popular reading of Indian famines represents what could be the default view. Before British rule, "in most of India water had *always* been a communally managed common resource."[9] According to such readings, sharing and cooperation were the ancient norms, and inequality and exclusion were the colonial inventions. The word "always" is significant. It stands for Indian culture, a good inheritance the colonial rulers destroyed, thus making famines more likely. These inferences, however, are untestable and questionable. Colonial property rights reform recognized ownership rights and left the right to the commons undefined. Because the state did not frame these rights in detail, the right to the commons would embed in cultural practice *even after* colonial property rules began. Did culture advocate inclusion, as the citation says, or exclusion, as the classical scholars would say?

Dumont is not in fashion among anthropologists anymore. Most historians and cultural anthropologists dealing with caste believe that some fundamental aspects of caste were created by colonial rule in the nineteenth century. An influential body of writings claims that village traditions, including the centrality of caste, were reinvented and coded during early colonial rule to make the village more intelligible.[10] The colonialists "fixed" Indian culture by a purposive reading of Indian data. The implication is that Indian culture was neither so permanent nor so hierarchical before as the colonialists imagined. All writings in the set use the word *fixing*, rarely in a precise sense.[11] The quality of historical research on precolonial social institutions is not robust either.

Historians studying a small region in Tamil Nadu have developed a detailed picture of water and rights in the early colonial times that support the reinvention idea. David Mosse shows how significant tanks were for cultivation in southern Tamil Nadu.[12] Mosse suggests that the early colonial rulers in Tamil Nadu believed that the maintenance of tanks by harnessing forced labor was a part of Indian tradition, whereas it was not so traditional. The claim, however, is about forced labor and not untouchability.

Was untouchability an invention or an inheritance? I cannot imagine that a caste-rights activist today would accept the idea that deprivation was a modern fiction. Ambedkar would treat the idea with contempt. He believed that the caste-sacredness link was an old one, entrenched in the Hindu worldview, and had nothing colonial about it. Indeed, the British rule in India had the promise of delivering justice by destroying that link; but, in the end, it proved too timid to do that.[13] Damodar Dharmananda Kosambi, a maverick theorist of Indian history, believed that the formation of "slave castes" was owed to climate more than religion. Frequent famines in the ancient past drove "aboriginals [to contract] away their freedom for bare but regular subsistence."[14] Freedom here means freedom to own assets like land or water. The statement highlights risk as part of Indian life and implies that acceptance of unfreedom reduced the risk. A historian and water activist rejects the notion that caste-based inequality in the access to natural resources was a colonial invention: "Indian peasant society was highly unequal even before the British came in. One source of this stratification is the caste system, which also blocked the entry of large sections of Indian rural society into landownership."[15] What is true of land should be true of water as well, for both were scarce resources.[16]

Whether ancient or not, around 1914, private or community rights to water bodies were not just a legal right but also a moral one. The moral command was under attack during the protest movements that emerged in the interwar period. These movements fell afoul of the authorities who believed it was their duty to protect the rule of law. The courtroom was the last resort. A case in 1914 is a good place to begin.

* * *

In 1914, Hiraman Dhondi Mochi drew water from a sacred lake affiliated to a temple near Bombay. A leatherworker and an untouchable, Mochi had concealed his caste identity when using the lake and posed as a fruit seller. When Mochi was found out, the temple authority sued him for having defiled the water. Insult to religion was an offense under penal law. The magistrate ordered a prison sentence. The case went to appeal and settled in Mochi's favor. The appellate court made a distinction between drawing water and intentional disrespect to religion, observing that if the two things conflated, all rivers would be inaccessible to most Indians.[17]

Whether as an effect of the judgment or the expansion of local self-government, in the next ten years, in many villages of western India, groups would try to take control of a pool held sacred by the upper castes. These cases did not end in violence or a court case but more often ended with arbitration of some sort. In a 1924 incident at the central Maharashtra temple town Lonar, the attempt by a "band of 500 untouchables" to "pollute the sacred stream" failed because the "Deputy Commissioner [had] threatened the depressed classes with instantaneous arrests in case they repeated their attempts."[18] A 1931 movement to open access to a well failed because of a dispute among the depressed caste groups. Caste set a moving target. "Within the ranks of 'untouchables,'" a newspaper report on a 1925 dispute said, "there are grades of untouchability, and where this is the case the higher grades will not drink from the wells of the lower grades."[19]

A yet third type of outcome was outsider arbitration, which was becoming more frequent in western India because M. K. Gandhi and Ambedkar tried to bring the depressed castes into the political mainstream, with different arguments. In 1931 in a Karnatak village, a political activist persuaded the upper castes to open access to the deprived castes; on condition, the latter would give up eating meat and drinking alcohol.[20] Ambedkar's *Annihilation of Caste* documented many more cases of local protest. Newspapers in the cities also recorded and discussed numerous instances wherein secure water, so far a private and community good guarded in the name of a shared social value, became a target of capture.

The most organized of the movements occurred in the small town of Mahad, one hundred miles south of Bombay, in 1927. A group led by Ambedkar tried to gain the right to draw water from a tank in the town. In 1927, the movement lost, but the matter went to court. In January 1931, a judge in the local court decreed that the Mahad town tank was public property and open to all.[21] From then on, Ambedkar's participation in the equality movement marked a departure in Indian political history.

B. R. (Bhimrao Ramji) Ambedkar (1891–1956) was born in an untouchable family from central India. His father was a major in the Indian army. The youngest of fourteen siblings, Ambedkar saw his life take an unusual turn when the princely ruler of Baroda state sponsored the education of the talented student, on condition that he would return to serve the Baroda state. That he did, and suffering segregation by his office colleagues, he left the service. The experience showed that an enlightened king alone was no match for social institutions. After that experience, he completed a law degree from London and returned to India in 1923. For the next twenty years, he mobilized lower-caste groups to campaign for equality. He wrested from the leaders of the nationalist movement a formal acknowledgment that the untouchables were a group outside of Hinduism and needed a separate electorate. He is now remembered more for that deed. In the public eye, the other persona, that of the first modern scholar of the caste system, is not so visible anymore. Many modern-day anthropologists of caste discard his understanding of caste. It was that understanding, challenging the notion of sacredness in Hinduism, that led him to mobilize a group to take water from a sacred tank.[22]

Western India was the center of the movement. In South India, the non-Brahmin movement in provincial politics had taken up the cause with less publicity.[23] In North India, caste difference entailed rules of sharing, but water was not such a scarce resource there. Conflicts emerged when religious reformers challenged these rules.[24] Provincial and princely state legislatures followed the incidents and court judgments and tried to keep in step. The princely state of Baroda passed a law depriving of government funds any organization practicing caste discrimination.

Even as they were on the retreat in the courtroom and the political stage, the backlash from upper-caste Hindus was fierce in the village.

* * *

There were many reports where some beat up others who had forced an entry into a public tank. Gandhi took up several such cases from coastal Gujarat.[25] In all of British India, a few district officers managed an enormous land and a large population. The officers understood that even if the law was starting to take the side of the depressed castes, a top-down order would not work as well as negotiations because the depressed castes were themselves divided and practiced water discrimination against each other.

In the Ahmadnagar District in 1934, the magistrate settled an intercaste dispute over wells by allocating these to both the upper and the depressed castes, but as soon as he left the scene violence broke out. Now the violence was among the depressed caste groups.[26] Similar clashes occurred in 1935 when a tank was declared open to all in a village in Mysore.[27] In the same year, a Hindu mob attacked a procession in Nashik, protesting against government inaction to ensure wider water access. The administration had few means to deal with a mob.[28] In 1938, riots broke out, and some people died in Bijnor (North India) over access to water.[29] Upper-caste violence was a risk to the upper-caste activists because of the threat of police action. Social boycott had no risk and was used to prevent access to wells on many occasions. One victim of such tactics was Laxmibai, a courageous woman from a Nagpur village who insisted on using the village well despite threats and faced a social boycott.[30]

Until 1919, the water campaign was not a mainstream political issue. After that, the political decentralization process made it more so, as I show next.

* * *

In 1919, provincial legislatures came up. In 1923, the Bombay Legislative Council passed a resolution that government grants would not be available for wells or land containing a pool unless all castes had equal access to these bodies. A series of incidents then followed where groups of people forced their entry into tanks situated on government land.

While the Mahad movement and many others like it momentarily failed, the pressure built on the provincial governments to act. The Bombay government was cash-short, but it did order that the waterworks or wells constructed by the district and local boards would not get grants "except on condition that the well or other work . . . [would be] available for the use of all castes and classes equally."[31] The announcements had a limited impact. A few years after the Mahad movement, in a report on the oppressed castes of Maharashtra, the sociologist M.G. Bhagat observed: "Nowhere have I found a common well used by the touchables [sic] and the untouchables, although from time to time, the Government might have issued orders, that all the public wells should be thrown open to all."[32]

More data were gathered on water access. The Bombay Backward Class Department, in its first annual report (1932–1933), surveyed the depressed castes' access to public goods. The report observed that in the villages, free access to water depended on the attitude of the district boards. The landholders often controlled these bodies. In the towns and the cities, the wealthy were not the landowning castes.

Law was a friend but an unreliable one. The campaign movements furthered the removal of caste-based access to public goods, and law helped. Not always, though. With water bodies where communities could claim a historic right of use, the law would exclude others. In 1933, in the developing northern suburbs of Bombay, the depressed castes' campaign to access a well used by the Christians and their Hindu employees led to an open battle. The Catholic priest in Vile Parle took the side of the depressed castes. So did the magistrate. The legal issue was complicated because papers existed to show that the well had initially been under private ownership. The municipality made piped water more accessible (for a fee) to those campaigning for access, and members proposed the construction of a separate well in the area.[33]

What, then, did the campaign achieve?

* * *

Between the two judgments—1914 about Mochi and 1931 about Mahad—case law had established an important principle: a source belonging to a public body (in the 1914 case a temple) was a public good. Together these incidents succeeded in making the struggle for equality a political issue. With an elected legislature taking over provincial governments in the interwar period, water equality could not be ignored anymore. "The events of 1927," writes the historian Anupama Rao about Mahad, "marked a significant departure in Dalit politics and inaugurated urban-centered regional associational forms."[34] According to Rao, the transformation of the untouchable into a Dalit (literally "oppressed"), a political subject, had begun. The year after the Mahad judgment, Gandhi's All India Antiuntouchability League formed. The figure of Ambedkar started to loom large in any discussion on equality, not least because of the caste reservation of electoral seats that he had helped achieve despite Gandhi's opposition.

On water, what did the movement achieve? The campaign had been successful in the cities, sporadically so in the countryside. In November 1932, participants in a seminar on equality held in Bombay observed that "there had been a remarkable change in the spirit of the people . . . in the cities" but not yet in the countryside, where "fear and . . . oppression" still prevailed.[35] The root of the difference was that water was more readily available in the cities, and piped water had reduced the predominance of private rights. In contrast, in the countryside, water was scarce, and the progress of public works was not enough to end the dominance of private rights.

Finally, the campaign had shown that it must use a range of weapons—law, media, public institutions, and the urban space. Cities, where the political axis of the movement was situated, were a more inclusive space because there was more water and more media presence there. The city was also better served with systems that delivered water in mass.

* * *

Until well into the second half of the nineteenth century, the technological-institutional setup involved in water supply in the cities looked quite similar to that in the countryside. Supplies came from ponds, lakes, and wells. "The poor low caste people," a report on Pune of 1872 said, "have . . . to wait at a little distance from the wells until some person of caste gives them, either for money or out of charity, a small quantity of water. There are very few wells in the city which are accessible to any but persons of caste, and there are hardly any wells at all which are not already dried up."[36] The mention of "for money" raises the interesting prospect that water markets emerged during shortages. While all markets tend to exclude the poor, markets could overcome caste distinctions. During the hot season in Bombay city, "water carts [went] about the town distributing scanty supplies here and there." Sold water did not meet the needs of the upper-caste people of the town. Their preferred option was still to own a well if they could fund it.[37]

Conditions were not different in Madras, indeed anywhere water still relied on common sources. A 1920s survey reported that untouchability was practiced in its most brutal and degrading forms in the city. Most people from the depressed castes had "no access to public wells, drinking water ponds, schools." These public goods created with public money were meant to be open to all. "But as Government recently admitted in the Legislative Council, there is very severe discrimination even in public institutions."[38]

And yet, access to opportunities did improve overall in the cities. The 1932 seminar mentioned before confirmed the point. The cities were becoming a more inclusive space for the depressed castes because there was a municipality funded with public money. One could buy water from the tap, mobilize many people, campaign for access in other ways, and get help from institutions like the church or political organizations. In small towns, the local administration worked on the principle that "the municipality should take steps for the protection of all tanks and public wells." "It is indeed one of their most important duties. There should always be a separate water-supply provided for low-caste people."[39] Barriers, however, could be weakened. In big railway stations, it was impossible to maintain caste and rank in such gatherings of strangers. Besides, the railways employed a considerable number of depressed caste people. "The Great Indian Peninsula Railway authorities have issued special instructions to the staff concerned to ensure that members of Depressed Classes are not debarred the use of wells or refused refreshment by the tea and food stall holders."[40]

To the extent these conditions were absent in the village, water access remained unequal there for much longer, and the campaign for access met with such violent reaction as to "seriously prejudice the existing rights of the Depressed Classes."[41]

* * *

After independence from British rule in 1947, the democratic state decided to make a difference. One of the first acts was the creation of a parliamentary committee on untouchability. Its report, leading up to the Untouchability (Offences) Act of 1955, repeatedly mentioned water, recommending that the denial of access on the religious ground be a criminal offense.

In many provinces where periodic aridity and caste-based inequality were of serious scale, the state governments spent a part of their budget for rural and community development on constructing wells for lower-caste people. After a massive turn toward rural infrastructure in the 1970s, piped water was extended in the countryside. Politicians in the Bombay and Madras Provinces underscored freeing access to water. In the colonial times, the officers could, in theory, suggest digging wells for the use of the depressed castes or in the localities where they lived. The village council, or panchayat, continued the practice after independence. A survey of panchayats in the Bombay Province observed that near Pune, the panchayat had allocated wells to Brahmins and non-Brahmins.[42]

The strategy worked, up to a point. The segregation of wells was not ideal. It would "perpetuate untouchability," whereas the ideal was "to [abolish it] as speedily as possible."[43] The right response was to persuade all castes to accept everyone's right to the common sources. Neither the officers nor the politicians had the means to implement such a change quickly. Therefore, discrimination continued even as investments poured into water supply.

In the Madras Province, improving the access of the depressed castes living in the villages fell upon several departments (irrigation, public works, Harijan Uplift) that did not work in coordination. Wherever there was a continued reliance on common sources, there was continued discrimination. In 1947, well over half of the municipalities in the Madras Province had a "protected" water supply scheme that the town authority operated. "The position in regard to rural water supply and sanitation is most pathetic. The villager and his essential needs have been grievously neglected; safe drinking water has been a rarity to him. The Harijans and their cheries [slums] are the worst sufferers in this respect."[44]

A quarter century after a nationwide community development program started, most villages had wells for the use of the depressed castes. In many, there was one well, and in none did the depressed castes have equal access to the well ordinarily used by the upper castes, though, in conditions of great scarcity, the upper castes did draw water from those the others used.[45] A survey of the 1970s found that more than half the population of the lower castes in the rural areas of Karnataka state could not use the public well or tank. The proportion was much smaller, at 15 percent, in urban areas.[46]

Similar levels of discrimination were reported from other states as late as the 1990s.[47] In the first decade of the twenty-first century, one estimate said that the women of oppressed caste households spent three hours every day gathering water for the family.[48] A 1990s survey found that whereas caste sentiment declined in most areas of life, water shortage aggravated it. "Untouchability is not experienced in normal times, but when water is scarce, the [oppressed castes] experience difficulty and discrimination in taking water from high caste localities."[49] With competition for water becoming intense, attempts to exclude others occurred often, and so did resistance and backlash against such moves. "For the past thirty years particularly," a book published in 2017 says, "Dalit assertions on water have accelerated."[50] Discrimination did not disappear.[51]

But the movement did achieve something lasting and significant. It killed the moral rule of purity. The present times are different from the world Ambedkar wanted to change. At the end of the twentieth century, the application of ritual purity had narrowed to fields such as temple access and did not work in water anymore.[52]

* * *

Most writings on Dalit political movements touch on the campaign for water access incidentally, as one issue among many the movement fought for. We would make a mistake to think that the battle for equal water rights was a campaign for equal rights in a generic sense. It was a *struggle for water*. The battle found meaning in a specific environment. It was not an accident that some of the driest areas of the Deccan, with a recent experience of famine, saw the emergence of the most influential political movement against orthodox Hinduism. A natural world exposing many to the threat of water famine was the fertile ground for such a struggle to develop. At the same time, in the two cities close to the region, Bombay and Pune, rights were debated and discussed, disputed in the courtroom, and tradition upheld and questioned. Whether caste and untouchability were colonial creation or not, the means to combat these forces were colonial creations. These were the courts, the mass media, the English press, and the legislature.

What did the movement for equal access to water achieve? It did not achieve real equality in water access everywhere, as the studies cited in the previous section suggest. There was upper-caste resistance. State authorities avoided confronting the resistance head-on. There was no nationalization of water sources and wells. The struggle for equality in water access, therefore, was a long-drawn-out one. What the movement did achieve was to destroy the religious ground for discrimination. The weapons in the battle were many, from the integration of the depressed caste movement into mainstream politics to the use of the press to conduct campaigns to claiming that water was a public good.

Chapter 4 is about the third step.

4

BECOMING A PUBLIC GOOD

Deep underground water belongs to the State in the sense that doctrine of public trust extends thereto. Holder of a land may have only a right of user and cannot take any action or do any deeds as a result whereof the right of others is affected.
—Supreme Court of India, 2004

The judgment from the top court has a tone of finality. It makes one think that a big problem was resolved, thanks to the enlightened judges. Such a reading would be hasty. The context for judgments like these (more will be discussed) is a geographical condition when all sources of water, both surface and underground, are monsoon-dependent. Increased use and fair distribution need to mind the capacity of the commons to recharge during the monsoon. If the balance is threatened, the state should step in. So far, so good. And yet, asserting the rule, a process begun in the late colonial times, was not easy. What about streams of water appearing in some seasons and disappearing in others? How can anyone assert a right over an impermanent asset? Local politics protects private rights to underground water, in which both the poor farmer and the affluent urbanite have a stake. Is a right to an aquifer of unknown features enforceable at all?

The journey of water rights from the private to the public has been tortuous and unfinished. The past 150 years have moved through three paradigms: recycling, impounding, and extraction. In the recycling model (roughly 1880–1930), the emphasis was on building canals and supplying treated water to the cities via pipes (chapter 5). The efforts succeeded in specific environments and not everywhere. In the impounding model (1930–1980), the accent was on river valley projects, especially in the dryland regions with a history of famines. Big dams built on rain-fed rivers became a high-maintenance, inequality-creating, and environmentally damaging pathway. In the extraction model (1980–), bore wells rule. Wells were always common in water-rich areas. In water-scarce ones, their role expanded after the 1980s. With these shifts, the governance of waterworks changed—from the private to the state and the community, back to private again. But during the last phase, a drive had built up to deliver all common sources to a custodian.

Chapter 3 described one kind of struggle initiated by social reformers and campaigners. The movement was about equality in usage. I now discuss the agency of the law and the state in protecting the sources. The recycling and impounding models figure a lot in this chapter.

Surface water bodies were the site for the deepest forms of legal, political, and technological intervention. Why was that the case?

* * *

Departing from indigenous practice, the British rulers of India defined proprietary right over natural resources as ownership right, as opposed to a user right, or usufruct (the right to enjoy the use of another person's property). The concept worked better in land than in water. Most water bodies, such as streams, lakes, or rivers, were common resources. They needed a custodian to manage the rights to use. Who should be the custodian? Rural communities were not the rightful custodians. Because these were unequal and divided, vesting control over resources to such communities would entail deprivation for many. In a caste-burdened society, the state—even a colonial state—was a fairer agent than the local community, although regulation by the state did not take all inequalities away and sometimes created new ones. More fundamentally, the law needed to recognize that water was a public good, access to which must be nonexclusive.

It was only in surface water that the idea had a chance. Groundwater was another matter. A well situated inside a homestead land was private property. Somewhere deep below the ground, an aquifer existed. No one owned it. There could not even be a custodian of a resource about which no one had a clear idea. In effect, for over a century, the state and law did not do anything about the wells. The green revolution and the rapid urbanization from the late twentieth century onward took advantage of the omission. As I show in chapter 6, the depletion of groundwater subsequently generated a struggle, to extricate groundwater from the sphere of private ownership and deliver it to a custodian. It is too early to be pessimistic, but the movement has not fared well so far.

To return to the past, rivers and lakes were long the main fields of experimentation with state-regulated water storage. Employees of the East India Company, which ruled over an expanding territory in India from 1765 to 1857, took that experimentation to a new level.

* * *

The early experiments had a definite character. The East India Company often projected itself as the just inheritor of Mughal or Maratha power. The company needed to show in what way it was an Indian kind of rule. And it did this by declaring water a priority for the state. By taking this step, the state was not serving welfare alone. Peasants being the main taxpayers, the state hoped to raise taxes by investing in water. The inheritance idea worked because past Indian regimes had left a network of canals, wells, dams, and aqueducts—much of it in ruins when the new state emerged. The engineers of the new state worked to expand the scale of these projects and build more along the same lines. Some, like Charles George Dixon (discussed below), departed from the Indian tradition. But they still stuck to local knowledge and resources. The company state could pursue such schemes on a bigger scale because it had more money power, thanks to a robust military machine. But money power served a traditional Indianist kind of engineering.

That changed after the Indian Mutiny of 1857, under three very different kinds of impetus. One of these was "bureaucratization" of irrigation management, or the expansion of the administrative infrastructure that enabled construction and maintenance of much larger systems than before and also the collection of water taxes from thousands of farmers. A second force was the application of European engineering ideas to India. The new ideas included silt control, basin management, and dam building on a much larger scale than the past Indian regimes did in hydraulics.[1] A third force took shape after 1900, when Indians took to civil engineering as a profession, and the subject was taught in Indian universities. With that transition, water schemes became tied to ideas of national development.[2] To this list, chapter 5 on the cities adds a fourth factor, municipalities or town administrations, which funded urban projects. These were not bureaucratic bodies but were elected by the wealthy residents. Merchants formed these bodies, and that shaped their functioning.

The colonial-era projects in surface water started in a small and local way. There were many examples. Two of these illustrate the nature of the enterprise. The first was in Pune, which, after it fell to the British in 1818, was the home of a large garrison. The town being located in the drier part of the peninsula, its water supply was insecure and fell short as the population rose. In 1858, the town had forty thousand people. Military engineers proposed schemes to improve supply. Most plans involved reviving the aqueducts inherited from the Maratha rulers. These projects—associated with names like Captain Jacob, Captain Graham, and Captain Kilner and those of two Parsi merchants, Vickajee Meerjee and Jamsetji—did not all materialize, but the correspondence about them unearthed a great deal of data on the indigenous systems.[3]

The second example occurs in an even drier region without a significant prehistory of large-scale water control. In 1836, Charles George Dixon (d. 1857), a lieutenant colonel in the Bengal Artillery, was appointed the superintendent of Ajmer-Merwara, a state in western India that fell into British hands at the end of the Maratha wars. Dixon's predecessors had to deal with insurgents. But Dixon ruled in peace and was in his post long enough to consider ways to improve the estate, which in his time meant a rise in population and revenue. The region bordered the great Thar Desert and was one of India's driest areas with human settlement. The memory of famine (1832) and emigration still fresh, he settled on a one-point improvement program. The first phase consisted of building wells with government money. But there was not enough subsoil water in all the terrain. The next part of the program involved trapping monsoon runoff in artificial lakes, a type of action that would now be called watershed management. When Dixon died, the improvement program was a success. Irrigated area had about doubled, and the land sustained a much larger population than when he began.[4]

In the decades after his death, engineers studied the South Indian artificial lakes, trying to find the formula that would show how deep the water should be to resist severe evaporation and whether the depth would be sustainable with the existing tools and the workforce. They researched the lakes the company had inherited from the past regimes and lobbied for new experimental lakes.[5] Arthur Cotton, who would lead the campaign for dams in deltaic South India, was a keen participant. So was Henry Conybeare of Bombay, who built reservoirs to supply water to the city. These engineers were an articulate set, water missionaries who treated Dixon as a pioneer.

Arthur Cotton (1803–1899) symbolized a transition from thinking locally to thinking on the scale of big ecological regions. Cotton, an engineer in the service of the Madras government, started on a small scale, reviving an old dam-cum-canals network on the Kaveri and the Coleroon Rivers in the Tanjore-Trichinopoly Districts. The project involved building short-height dams to impound and redirect water flow. When these proved a success in raising taxes, he persuaded the authorities to build similar works on the mouths of the Godavari (1847–1852) and the Krishna. These later works, some finished by others, changed the game in many ways. These were enormous, much bigger than the Kaveri-Coleroon works. And these did not build on prior foundations. The capital cost, therefore, was high, and the returns low. And because there was no prior history, these works had a revolutionary impact on the countryside. The canals stimulated commodity trade, diversification into profitable water-intensive crops, and small-scale industries such as oil, rice, tobacco, and sugar factories. These activities concentrated in small towns that grew larger, like Vijayawada, Eluru, Rajahmundry, Kakinada, and Vizagapatam (Visakhapatnam). The bulk of India's tobacco crop came to be produced in the nearby Guntur District. The two deltas, ravaged by the Guntur famine in 1833, led a green revolution after 1860.

A third such region was the present-day western Uttar Pradesh and Haryana states, where a network of canals emerged in the nineteenth century. The network used in part disused channels created by the Indo-Islamic states that had ruled the region from the thirteenth century until the rise of the East India Company rule in the late eighteenth century. These canals were the cherished projects of Proby Cautley (1802–1871), an army officer. More an engineer (and paleontologist) than a military man, Cautley planned to draw, and partly resurrect, several hundred miles of channels off the Ganges and the Jumna. Initially, it received little support from the government. The engineering work became more challenging because of that fact. Cautley and his team managed the project hands-on, which involved, among other tasks, dealing with thousands of artisanal bricklayers. The project finished in 1854, eighteen years in the making. At its end, the irrigation lobby had divided into two, one devoted to Cautley and the other one led by Cotton, who thought the Ganges-Jumna project had defects.

* * *

In Punjab, the canal principle worked on a far more ambitious scale. Before 1850, Punjab was an arid area containing a vast savanna that supported pastoralism but little cultivation. Monsoon rains died away in the western part of the region, and intensive agriculture was possible only close to the rivers or in narrow strips watered by wells. The area, however, had large perennial rivers that formed in the Himalayas. The most successful ruler of pre-British Punjab, Ranjit Singh, had understood the potential value of these rivers and constructed canals using the water. Before his reign, the rural population of Punjab lived in low-lying plains along the rivers. These tracts either had well irrigation or enough rainfall. Much of the region, however, was too arid for agriculture. Ranjit Singh arranged to construct (in some cases revive) several inundation channels taken from the rivers.[6] Besides being seasonal in operation, the canals watered the area around the rivers, which already had well irrigation.

When Punjab was annexed to British India (1846–1849), the idea of canals was already there, and the need to develop irrigation over a wider area to give employment to a vast number of disbanded soldiers became a political necessity.[7] However, one thing was needed to convert that idea into a project serving a much larger area than anything built before. As with the lakes, the missing piece was scientific data to assure the engineers that canals, in effect human-made rivers, would be sustainable in the face of severe evaporation.

In the 1840s, engineering projects were a business of the army. In 1848–1849, a group of army officers and engineers stationed in Punjab during a military campaign observed that a canal network was possible. When the last major battle in

Anglo-Sikh wars, Chilianwala, was over, Lieutenant Richard Baird Smith wrote a pamphlet about "opening up" Punjab to British commerce and doubling the revenue of the province. Canals would be the stone killing the two birds. Baird Smith (1818–1861), a Scottish army officer, lived in India from 1836 until his death in Madras. He played a large role in two big conflicts, the Anglo-Sikh wars, and the Indian Mutiny-cum-rebellion. More than the battles, the experience of working with Proby Cautley on the Ganges-Jumna canals between 1841 and 1843 consumed his considerable mental energy. With that experience behind, the report was precise about the feasibility of controlling and rechanneling the flow of river water.

Between 1870 and 1920, engineers built canals tapping the waters of the five rivers of Punjab. The canals turned the interfluvial tracts, which earlier sustained pastoralism, into arable land. Nine "canal colonies" created out of these irrigation projects appeared. The projects irrigated 2 million hectares. The earliest colony was Sidhnai, and the last the Nili Bar. The largest were Lower Chenab (800,000 hectares) and Lower Bari Doab and Nili Bar (400,000 hectares each). The length of canals taken from Himalayan rivers in Punjab increased from 2,700 miles to more than 17,000 miles, enabling a rise in cultivable land from 27,000 to over 40,000 square miles.

Canals weakened traditional ritualistic inequality. Most beneficiaries of the canals were not from the upper castes of Hindu society. And yet, canals caused another kind of inequality to grow. Access to canal water was an asset. The farmer who had it was better-off than someone who had the same amount of land but no access to a canal. The response to economic inequality was to build more. The state lost the capacity to build more after World War I. Staring at bankruptcy, the empire had no stomach to sustain the building drive. After independence in 1947, canals received a new impetus, now as tools for the economic development of the new nation.

* * *

After 1947, the government invested big in building canals. The immediate impetus to expand the canal system came from the partitioning of Punjab into two parts, one in Pakistan and the other in India. Punjab canals were an impressive system, but by 1940, they did not meet the demands of the four million hectares of irrigated land that had come into existence. The Himalayan rivers did carry water throughout the year. In winter, however, the level dropped enough to starve the canal system. "Vast quantities of water go to waste in the summer, but there is not enough to go round in the winter."[8] Canals were beginning to be run only in winter, with limited effect. Where they could, Punjab farmers borrowed money to dig wells. Still, at the time of independence of India and Pakistan, the demand for water in the canal colonies exceeded the capacity of the system.

The Partition of India created a further complication. The sources for all the five Punjab rivers were in India, whereas four of the five basins occurred mainly in Pakistan territory. Both countries were committed to expanding the system's capacity because resettling peasant migrants was of great urgency. Both countries had limited options to plan such expansion. India acted on the Bhakra Dam project, first proposed in 1919, to impound the Sutlej and extend the Sirhind Canal to a larger area. Pakistan was keen to build reservoirs in the upper valleys, which included Kashmir.

This initial boost was then followed by a massive investment in the upland rivers in southern and eastern India. A resolve to end poverty in any manner had made the developmental agenda overlook the potential costs of irrigation projects, as "overriding priority was mostly placed on the first-order effects of technology and economic growth."[9] The 1970s green revolution further endorsed the investment in canals. By 1990, there were over two thousand dams across Indian rivers. Most of these had appeared in the Deccan region, where there was less water overall, yet the topography permitted storage more easily than in the flat Indo-Gangetic basin.

Canals weakened caste-based inequality. But legislation was necessary for other forms of storage to achieve equality.

* * *

Canals were an egalitarian resource in a sense, more than wells. In access to irrigation water, caste was not as significant a factor as access to drinking water, and its importance receded further after independence. Lloyd I. Rudolph and Susanne Hoeber Rudolph called the smallholding beneficiaries of land reforms (the 1950s) and green revolutions (the 1970s and 1980s) the "bullock capitalists." Most bullock capitalists were of low ritual status. "The political coming of age of bullock capitalists . . . is strengthened by the first wave of the so-called backward classes movement in the northern Hindi Heartland states and Gujarat and the second wave in the southern and western states."[10] In the hierarchy documented by the colonial officers, these castes ranked above the "untouchables" but below so-called upper castes. A process of agrarian change empowering groups like these also helped to reduce caste-based water access.

Along with the democratization of access to water, the law recognized water as a public good. British Indian law was ambiguous on the right to the commons. The rule defined private property differently from previous regimes. It defined it as an ownership right rather than as a right to use an asset. Access to the commons required setting out rules of use rather than ownership, which was left incomplete. A variety of consequences followed from the inconsistency. Peasants sometimes grabbed village commons.[11] More often, a sharp division came into being between nomads, pastoralists, and forest-dependent peoples who *used* resources and the peasants, planters, and landlords who *owned* resources.

This inconsistency was present in water too. British Indian law left the right to groundwater to the owner of the land where a well or a pond was situated. The water from a river was not fixed on space. Mainly via the Indian Easements Act of 1882, the law recognized private and communal rights over surface water. Easement, however, was no solution to settling the right to transient forms of surface water and often raised more problems than it solved.

Easement right is a right to access another person's property for the "beneficial enjoyment" of one's property. For example, an agricultural land is partitioned so that a well falls in one part. The owner of the other part could claim access to the well without having a property right on the land on which it exists. Easement rights could also apply to the cases where the mode of use of one person's property causes problems for a neighbor, for example, when sewage water released by one home passes through the courtyard of the neighbor's house.

The Indian Easements Act of 1882, in principle, enabled one to make a case for access to a water source someone else could claim as a property. The use of the act to settle water rights cases was rare in the Indian courts until 1910. On the one hand, those that did appear affirmed the right of the landowner to water bodies in the land owned (*Thayammal v. Muttia*, Madras High Court, 1887). On the other hand, the right of the city authority to acquire property belonging to others "for the purpose of supplying the city with water" was confirmed in an 1890 suit in the Bombay High Court (*Great Indian Peninsula Railway v. Bombay Municipal Corporation*).[12]

Cases were rare because the act excluded underground water from its scope. Wells, therefore, were rarely disputed. In several partition-of-property cases, the right to a well so far used by an extended family was at stake (*Janardan Mahadeo Bhase v. Ramchandra Mahadeo Bhase*, Bombay High Court, 1926). The easement case was that all extended family members should continue to have access to the well. Should the right, however, cease when a member sold the share, left the place, or transferred land ownership to a new owner? On questions like these, the Easements Act, which favored sharing of the commons, and property inheritance acts, which favored the idea of the unity of family property (or exclusion of outsiders), were at odds. In *Ramaswami and others v. Muniswami and others* (Madras High Court, 1959), the right to well water was broadened under the Easements Act, meaning a landowner who needed to use a well in another land or formerly did so could claim the right to use. However, where the pattern of use was in doubt, wells remained excluded from the act's scope.

Surface water raised further complications. As cultivation expanded and the population grew, a class of suits appeared in the High Courts involving the application of easementary right to flowing water that did not classify as streams or rivers. These suits debated the nature of the right of owners of non-riparian land over moving water of any kind, whether rainwater or channels taken from rivers and canals. Almost always, these cases involved someone who, situated on the pathway of water, erected a barrier to its flow.

A more complicated scenario involved the monsoon rainwater used for irrigation or other purposes. It was, in theory, easier to deal with the inequality when someone situated at the upper reaches of a river had access to more water than one located at a lower reach of the river, partly because such inequality appeared everywhere and had many cases to serve as precedents. But then, the river is a permanent body of water. What about impermanent bodies? A vast quantity of rainwater was trapped for use for a season. Everyone tried to do that, if possible. Rainwater flows down a slope. The user at the upper reaches of the slope could trap more water, but, quite often, those at the lower reaches had some recorded customary right to its use. The custom was one thing, and formal law was another. With a seasonal stream, when there was a dispute, the inspection party appointed by the court might not even find the stream, let alone settle rights. Rights over impermanent bodies were coming under debate because the land through which rainwater would pass had meanwhile been acquired as private property. In *Sitaram Motiram v. Keshav Ramchandra* (Bombay High Court, 1945), the appeals court settled that no easement right could exist with rainwater. However, disputation did not end.[13]

Quite a different way to ensure water equity was to declare a resource as public property. Law again was hesitant about doing this.

* * *

The courts sanctioned an eminent domain rule from the interwar period, whereby the state could take over a common water source "in the public interest." Years before, the

Northern India Canal and Drainage Act of 1873 had empowered the state to "use and control for public purposes the water of all rivers and streams" and lakes of natural origin. Like this act, the application of eminent domain, where the state could override custom, was limited to a few provinces until 1947. Still, it established an important principle: surface water was a public good as opposed to groundwater.[14] There is little research available to suggest the exact motivations leading to these laws. Probably, the inspiration came from the irrigation projects and the famine experience. However, no single rule of law emerged since water was a provincial subject and the provinces often competed for water.

Since 2000, the gathering water stress generated a discussion on the history of property right in water and the nature of the right.[15] These writings show why the judicial and political process often failed to deal with water stress. From a present-day perspective, laws relating to water use in India look like a "patchwork."[16] A hesitant assertion of public trust in overground sources and the tenacity of private rights in underground sources would confirm the impression. Land reforms in India in the 1950s, which were meant to reduce landlord power, left intact the power of the landowners who had access to secure groundwater. Patchy legislation left behind these anomalies.

Further, the eminent domain rule became controversial in the late twentieth century when the state asserted the right to allocate water from common sources to industry. It also failed to resolve potential disputes about one province's claim to another province's water. An unresolved issue of principle underlay these contests. How would state-mediated redistribution work when the people who relied on a common water source had conflicting interests? And how did state mediation work in a federal setup where provinces had contradictory interests?

Although it might seem like a patchwork, India's environmental law does fall in a pattern. The perception of the problem has a definite center. The challenge at an earlier time was ensuring fair distribution. The challenge now is the potential depletion of a common property resource that depends, like everything else, on monsoon rainfall. The caste and equality battle was India's own. Once the problem was defined as the reduction of a shared pool, the Indian jurisprudence could follow global thinking on environmental law, as I discuss next.

* * *

Over the last quarter of the twentieth century, the axis of discourse on water changed from insecurity to depletion. In turn, depletion could mean overuse and absolute decline in the quantity available or pollution and a decline in the quality available. In all three cases—restricted access, fall in quantity, and fall in quality—a person harmed has a "standing" to file a suit for redressal. Under what law would one seek redressal?

One approach to dealing with a fall in quantity or quality is to invoke the "harm" caused to humans and compensate. The concept of harm is too human-centric and turns on finding a practicable definition of "harm," which is neither easy nor obvious. There is another problem with the compensation principle. Where there is the pollution of a river, the individual with an existing legal interest in the river's waters can bring a suit claiming the polluter has violated rights. The petitioner may be compensated in a settlement. But the environment will still suffer a fall in quality. And those individuals who have a customary or legally weak user right continue to be denied access to enough good water. Another approach is needed to make the river itself or the "public" at large the beneficiary of a legal remedy.

In environmental law, the public trust doctrine structures laws about the public use of natural resources. As I have shown in chapter 2, the public trust doctrine emerged in India during famine operations, more in administrative practice than in law. The public trust principle—the state should hold in trust some natural elements like lakes or rivers—can be applied on different grounds. One of these is "natural purpose"; for example, the natural purpose of a lake is to be a lake rather than a garbage dump. A second one is rational management. Many judgments using the doctrine in the US referred to the "rational management" of natural resources, meaning economizing the use of a scarce and useful resource. A third ground yet is sustainability, the fear that the commons would be overused and destroyed without public trust. A fourth one is historical usage, when, for example, the enclosure of a beach in use by the public for a long time is rejected. A fifth ground yet is that some natural elements, whether the enjoyment of a mountain scene or the life-giving properties of underground water, cannot be excluded from anyone.

Water lends itself to the fifth, or non-excludability, dimension of the public trust doctrine readily because, unlike land, all water comes from common pools, and water saves lives. Such reasoning can override past private property in water on the basis of an inadequate understanding of the commonness of underground water. Commonness gives rise to "the rule of water law that one does not own property right in water in the same way he owns his watch or his shoes, but that he owns only usufruct—an interest that incorporates the needs of others."[17]

In India, the public trust argument has been used more often recently, though few significant cases deal with water. In one landmark judgment related to a public park in Lucknow town, where a private right was allowed against historical usage, the Supreme Court invoked public trust to overturn the decision.[18] In 1997, a Supreme Court case affirmed a notion, present since colonial times, that the state was the trustee for the water in the commons.[19] The ruling made a state-mediated allocation of common sources for private uses difficult. The Supreme Court cited Joseph L. Sax, the environmental law expert, in a 1997 case concerning forest lands (*M. C. Mehta v. Kamal Nath*). In 2002–2003, a Coca-Cola bottling plant in Kerala faced closure after a court acceded to the campaigners' argument that the plant affected the area's water resources adversely. The Supreme Court reaffirmed the public trust doctrine to "deep" underground water in *State of West Bengal v. Kesoram Industries Ltd. and others* (2004). The citation at the head of the chapter comes from the judgment. No restrictions on the state's right would be absolute, the court explained.

Several countries in the world have passed laws making the right to water a fundamental right. The right to water is not an environmental law, nor does it have implications for trusteeship. But the assertion of such a right can have an environmental effect if the right is invoked to resist pollution and overuse by others. That is, if it is asserted in the form of a dual right: I should have access, and others should not deny me access.

The Water (Prevention and Control of Pollution) Act in India, passed in 1974 and long dormant, has been since 2000 a rallying point for several hundred cases, which asserted such a dual right. At the same time, interpretations of Article 21 of the Constitution of India—"No person shall be deprived of his life or personal liberty except according to procedure established by law"—have treated the right to safe and clean drinking water as a fundamental constitutional right. The concern with "safe and clean" suggests that the inclusion of the right into the set of fundamental rights derives from public health considerations rather than equity ones. Indeed, the discussion around such a right has been oblivious to the long history of the struggle to access water equality that chapter 3 described. Instead, the focus in contemporary discussions falls on health. The meaning of "safe and clean" varies from one government department to another and between the courtroom and the scientific community, which makes the right of doubtful value.[20] Cross-country evidence remains mixed on whether having such a law makes a difference to broader or more equitable access to water.[21]

A second approach to addressing overuse is granting nature the status of a legal person with a distinct set of rights mimicking some but not all the rights a real person has.[22] Then, the harm caused to nature would become a ground for legal remedy. Companies and charities have been recognized as a person with rights. Why not nature? In an influential paper, Christopher D. Stone set out three conditions needing to be fulfilled for natural objects to have a legal persona: the possibility of legal action if the object were threatened, the possibility to perceive threats to the object independently of threats to others dependent on it, and the possibility of action that would remedy the threat to the object.[23]

This approach can work with rivers. Geographical complexity, and the facts that the river flows through many territories and the water is not a fixed resource and therefore not easy for one regulator to protect, makes a legal rather than an administrative approach more attractive. The solution still entails the presence of a custodian or trustee since rivers, like minors, "cannot speak for themselves." The custodian should be independent and with enough financial capacity to conduct inquiries and enforce its orders. Giving rivers legal rights can reduce political interference or conflicts of interest. In a land where a sizable human population lives on rivers, the life of a river and the lives it sustains are interdependent.

The first-ever application of the principle was not promising for India. In March 2017, the High Court of Uttarakhand declared the Ganges and the Jumna rivers as legal persons (Ganga and Yamuna, respectively), on the grounds, among others, that they were sacred and, therefore, harm to the rivers amounted to harm to religion.[24] The judgment settled two cases, one protesting illegal encroachments on the riverbank and the other about the conduct of industrial activity polluting the waters. The damage the industrial and consumer use caused to these two rivers of the Indo-Gangetic basin is the subject of an immense literature and an energetic field of activism, as I have shown. The judgment, however, was unprecedented and had huge implications if it became a case law.

Not long after, the Uttarakhand government filed an appeal in the Supreme Court, saying that its role as a custodian was unclear since the rivers flowed through other territorial units. Besides revealing complexities regarding the juristic personhood concept, the outcome raised new questions about how far religion could aid environmental causes. If religion were to be a ground to protect nature, could it justify destruction of nature, say, by permitting cremation on the riverbank? Would a judgment like the High Court's encourage religious revivalism? Could the spiritual argument be used to stop development projects that may not harm the river? Most such questions arose from the reference to sacredness in the judgment. The jurisdictional issue the government raised was a distinct one and had broader implications for the use of personhood for other rivers in the future.

Since the conventional courts were overburdened with traditional cases, the Indian government has introduced, in several fields, parallel courts of justice. The process is expected to reduce the length of the proceedings. Since 2010, the National Green Tribunal has heard environmental law cases.[25] The cases involving water have been few, and nearly all dealing with the pollution of rivers. It is too early to say if the tribunal is making a difference. However, the use of the tribunal suggests a sense of urgency attaching to perceptions about the commons.

* * *

The chapter describes the emergence of an idea of "the public," at first via irrigation projects, then via the law of access to the commons. In both fields where the rights to water were redefined, the process was chaotic and unplanned. A deep root for the chaos was impermanent streams and unknown aquifers.

Many towns and cities did not face these issues. Assertion of the public good principle was easier in the cities. Chapter 5 discusses how the shift came about.

5

WATER IN THE CITIES

Thirsty Indian cities have a management problem, not a water problem.
—*The Economist*, 2019

The site of the equality campaign (chapter 3) was the village. The cities were a different world. The port cities were constrained neither by water shortage nor by seasonality. No one died there of thirst. Because life was more secure in the seaboard cities, those like Bombay, Calcutta, and Madras received many migrants. Their high population growth from time to time created local water shortages and epidemics. Calcutta was among the wealthiest and most water-abundant cities in the early nineteenth century. Yet, a Bengali doctor in 1850 "[did] not see in the town of Calcutta any children that [were] in perfect health," for all lived on contaminated water.[1] Water channels inside the cities degenerated with population pressure. The neglect of water supply and drainage increased malaria and cholera in the densely settled areas where the new migrants lived.

In part, the quality problem was owed to an urban type of inequality. In the nineteenth century, the richer towndwellers lived on private wells, and the poorer people lived on common sources. Those owning a well had water throughout the year. Everyone else was exposed to seasonal fluctuations. But then, over time, private wells were overused as families grew and employed many servants. Enteric diseases, therefore, did not spare the well-off either.

In the port cities, the public health drive started with water supply projects. Sanitation, disease control, and a centralized supply of water became interconnected goals. The cities could meet that aim more effectively than the village, thanks to a combination of three urban features that remained missing elsewhere. First, engineers had more say in administration. Second, the principle of self-government was tried in the municipal authority early, so that rich merchants ran the city. Whether from altruism or fear of their own safety, they had the motivation, as well as the means, to fund big projects. The third factor was the ease with which a corporate entity could work in a city, to own utilities such as filtration and coagulation lakes and a network of pipes and faucets. Many towns and cities shared some of these features. Still, they were not alike. Dry South India posed more significant challenges than the wet eastern India. All still overcame obstacles.

For at least one hundred years since these projects began, the urban systems relied on recycling and impounding monsoon water (chapter 4). As the strategy's capacity came under pressure due to explosive urbanization, groundwater took over as the new paradigm at the end of the twentieth century. A newly rich class of apartment owners solved their water problem by digging deep wells. The rapid rise in the private use of underground water meant slackening of regulation too. Such absence of regulation is the "management problem" the citation at the start of the chapter referred to.

The port cities of colonial India were not only centers of commercial and military power but also sites where large waterworks were erected. How did that activity start?

* * *

Bombay, Madras, and Calcutta had a common origin in the British East India Company enterprise and its need for bases secure from potential attacks by Indian rulers and European rivals. When these settlements began in the mid- to end of the seventeenth century, they were nothing more than overgrown villages. Where Calcutta arose, there was a seasonal marketplace of some sort before, but nothing of a scale to foreshadow the center of global commerce and industry that Calcutta would become around 1900. As warfare broke out inland and the Mughal Empire and the successor states became less attractive as business destinations beginning in the late eighteenth century, there was a steady influx of Indian merchants, bankers, artisans, and workers into these cities. The cities were still not secure places. The ruler of Bengal invaded Calcutta in 1756. Madras was lost to the French for some time. In the end, British power survived, and the cities continued to draw Indian immigrants in the nineteenth century.

In 1857–1858, as the mutiny broke out in the Indo-Gangetic basin and turned into a civil rebellion in several towns, the port cities stayed peaceful. The merchants and bankers expressed support to the regime. Their support made the three port cities handy instruments in battling the rebellion. Directly, the cities played a somewhat limited role in territorial conquest, for geographical and communication barriers kept the seaboard and the interior quite separate until the railways brought them closer. The port cities played a vital role in politics in an indirect way, by being centers of naval power and by being magnets to the wealthy elite from Indian society. The elite had their interests. Some saw in the East India Company an agent to better serve their economic ambitions than the old feudal chiefs of the interior. Others saw in it an agent creating institutions, which would deliver useful education and a cosmopolitan cultural milieu to their children.

There was another unique advantage of the three port cities and the seaboard in general: water security. Most seaboard cities did not suffer from a water shortage as severe as the interior regions did. The port cities were not water-scarce. They received higher rainfall on average. They were situated on estuaries and deltas where there was a constant water flow even in rivers that shrank in the summer. They could grow because they provided food and water to more people.

Discussions around the notion of "monsoon Asia" (chapter 1) observe that the concept did not explain the economic history of Singapore and Hong Kong well. It did not because services and not agriculture were the economic foundation of many seaboard cities. The trade-and-finance-based cities did not see such sharp seasonal effects as the agriculture-based countryside did. Trade and finance were the main occupations in the Indian maritime towns too. Before 1850, trade and finance in the port cities did respond to the seasonality effect, for shipping needed to use the monsoon winds and avoid the monsoon storms. Steamships later were less reliant on monsoon winds and more able to withstand violent weather.

Outside the port city, towns had limited capacity to provide water. India's urbanization ratio was low and stagnant until the mid-nineteenth century. There was nevertheless a reshuffle between the interior and the coasts. It began in the mid-eighteenth century. For the next seventy or eighty years, the three ports the East India Company owned (a fourth, Karachi, joined them in the 1840s) grew fast in population. In contrast, several cities in the formerly Mughal-ruled Indo-Gangetic basin depopulated.[2] The reshuffle was an effect partly of political shifts and partly of the growth of Indo-European maritime trade in goods like indigo and opium. After 1850, technological change aided the process. The volume of rail-borne trade increased. Port cities were a clearinghouse for the trade. Carrying the produce of many regions meant that the railways were busy throughout the year since local crops did not all follow identical seasonal cycles. Thus, if the seaboard had been less susceptible to the water constraint from before, it also had the means to overcome seasonality and do business all year-round.

Because it did, urban business growth and agricultural growth started to diverge at the end of the nineteenth century. Between 1900 and 1945, real income in industry and services increased by 133 percent, and real income in agriculture by 26 percent. In the same period, income per worker in manufacturing and services increased by 180 percent, and income per worker in agriculture increased by 6 percent.[3] The mainstay of business growth was long-distance commodity trade. Cargo carried by the railways and the ports increased from 5 to 140 million tons between 1871 and 1939. Finance and banking expanded to support the growth. Merchants and trading firms invested trading profits in cotton and jute textile factories. Migration increased. And migration had the effect of reducing the extent of seasonal unemployment. The impulse was urban-biased.

And yet, about 1850, the port city was no more than a village in the matter of water supply. Most of the wealthy residents had their homestead wells. Most of the poorer residents relied on ponds, lakes, and streams. The average volume of water available in these sources was somewhat higher than back in the villages where the poorer residents came from. Still, the water was seasonally variable, of poor quality, and often fell short as more migrants arrived.

In the army's engineering corps, there were advocates of gravity schemes that had found an application in the enormous canal projects. Army officers were concerned about water because the barracks suffered from frequent cholera outbreaks. Cholera broke out in the cities too. Many people doubted how receptive the Indian quarters of the cities would be to the idea of a common tap and to paying a tax to get it. The resistance notwithstanding, the cities did develop gravity systems and piped water, thanks in part to the growing economic and political power of businesspersons and in part to a moral concern originating in Britain and migrating to different parts of the empire. "At home and abroad," writes a historian of urban water supply in colonial India, "rulers and reformers identified the same practical problems, the unhygienic habits of the working class or native city dweller, and the same abstract predicament, the moral degeneration of townspeople living among 'filth,' and applied the same environmental solutions."[4]

How did the change come about? Depending on local environments, the history of municipal water projects would vary.

* * *

Between 1830 and 1860, Bombay's population increased from 250,000 to 670,000. An island, the city had not much land to grow on. The settlement pattern was segregated between garden houses for the affluent and crowded neighborhoods for the rest. Most Indians of modest means lived in these neighborhoods. Almost all of the migration and population growth happened there. The Europeans and the wealthy Indian merchants built homes near gardens and open spaces. The densely populated districts housed workers, artisans, and small traders. Until 1860, the wealthier families owned wells, and the poor and the middle-class ones relied on rivers, streams, and tanks. The rapid rise in population density reduced the average water access for all. In the summer months, the scarcity was acute. Thus, water shortage threatened Bombay's future as a commercial city. Sanitation was a matter of great worry because of the prevalence of waterborne diseases.

Bombay received heavy monsoon rains. The watershed had numerous seasonal streams that could, in theory, be trapped or dammed to create lakes. The solution to the periodic scarcity and bad-quality problems was transporting piped water from human-made and natural lakes into storage tanks in the city. The sanitary reformers campaigned for such a project. One of them, whose authority belied his age, was Henry Conybeare (1823–1892). Initially employed in the team creating the first railway line in India, Conybeare was an outstanding civil engineer and had a creative mind. He designed a Gothic church (the Afghan Church) in the town and persuaded the authorities to spend money on a water supply scheme. The first stage of the plan was completed in 1863–1864 when water from the Vihar Lake entered the city. Conybeare had already left for England.

Governor Henry Bartle Frere (1815–1884) gave municipal administration the institutional setup it needed to sustain such large-scale works. A key element in the initiative was to involve the city's Indian merchants in public activities. Frere was acting not only in an official capacity. An accomplished scholar of Indian history and languages, and with a history of disagreements with both the imperial authority and Indian Brahmins on policy matters, Frere commanded an image of impartiality. His campaign for self-government for the port city found powerful allies among the Indians. In 1865, the first municipality with the required legislation had come into being. Although Frere's efforts received a shock in the economic crash the city suffered the next year, the town now had an executive authority of its own, and water was the first field of action it engaged in.[5]

That was the start of a new set of troubles. Municipal finances raised corruption scandals almost from the beginning. There was strong resistance to paying the water tax. "So warm was the discussion in 1868 that there were not wanting members of the Corporation who . . . talked of the water rate as a 'confiscation.'"[6] Some of these critics were residents who owned private wells and did not worry about their situation. Others believed they were paying too much to cover up corruption and extravagance.[7] The policy did not reverse, but its pursuit generated more quarrels.

As water access improved, sanitation emerged as a bigger problem. More piped water without efficient drainage and sewage raised the risk of new diseases, like malaria. Bombay's growing population lived in different sanitary conditions. For "Bombay's urbanization was badly imbalanced in wealth and numbers between the prosperous and the poor."[8] The plague at the turn of the twentieth century was a reminder of inequality. The slums had neither a proper waste disposal system nor adequate drainage, and people lived too close to one another. The exact causal links between sanitation and plague remain a debated issue. Most British health officers then believed that unsanitary living conditions caused the plague. Some plague experts researching rat fleas believed in a different theory of the origin of the epidemic. It was still likely that stagnant water and poor waste disposal made the fleas breed fast or that many cases of pneumonic, as opposed to bubonic, plague spread because of the crowded living conditions.

Still, Bombay's projects were an engineering success and made a huge contribution to human welfare. Between two years, 1872 and 1881, the population of the Bombay Presidency stayed around 23 million, not changing at all because of the 1876–1878 famine.[9] The population of the city increased in the same decade by 20 percent, from 644,405 to 773,196. Many among these additions to the city's population were migrants fleeing from water- and food-scarce areas in the interior. In the next famine decade, 1891–1901, the population in both the presidency and the city fell by 6 percent, in the presidency because of the 1896 and the 1898 famines and in the city because of a plague epidemic. After that, Bombay's population bounced back, rising 26 percent in the next decade and faster than the presidency for years after that.

What do these data tell us? In one account, high plague mortality among the poorer inhabitants of the city tells us that "the city's rampant, vigorous uncontrolled development encouraged social Darwinism. . . . The successful prospered, lived well generally, monopolized wealth and flourished, while the larger number of ordinary inhabitants suffered and perished inordinately."[10] The rather one-sided assessment overlooks that the plague was a price paid for the city's attraction for people fleeing famine conditions in the interior. The

1872–1881 rise of the city's population when many people inland perished shows that the lives of the poor were better protected in the city. The huge bounce back in 1901–1911 indicates the city's ability to provide jobs and basic needs.

Thus, a city with little natural advantage to boast of except a good harbor experienced population growth, industrialization, and commercialization from 1870 onward. The population was spread out over a larger area inland. From less than 700,000 in 1870, the city was home to a million people in 1910, 3 million in 1950, and 4 million in 1960. More reservoirs had been added to the water infrastructure in the first half of the twentieth century. Still, the city administration tended to fall behind in the race. In 1941–1951, per head water availability fell from seventy gallons to about half the level.[11]

There is truth, then, in "uncontrolled development." None knew it better than the town administration. Large-scale projects solved the water problem. Drainage, sewage, and sanitation were not always amenable to large-scale intervention. Every burst of migration reduced the per capita availability of basic amenities. A 1939 report on town governance in Bombay showed that the sanitation problem persisted for a legal reason. The land was privately held. A part of the sanitation process, the clearance of human wastes, was decentralized to the holder of the property right. Most houses for the poor did not have toilets. As migration grew, and rents increased, landlords neglected their civic duties and avoided extra expenditure. "The people," stated the report, "ease themselves anywhere . . . [t]here is hardly any arrangement for water supply or drainage . . . the huts have neither plinths nor windows, and they are generally over-crowded. The landlord's only concern is to send his servant to collect the rents, and he does not care for the sanitation of the premises."[12] These accounts do not tell us that the poor in the city suffered. Instead, migrants deprived of water in the village found it in the city. And because they did, sanitation and disease became such serious problems.

The method differed in Calcutta, but the purpose was the same.

* * *

The first major waterwork in Calcutta was erected in 1870. Before the Calcutta Waterworks Company came into existence, to look after the project, "the water-supply of Calcutta [had] . . . been a mixture of surface-drainage and street-washings, collected in open tanks."[13] The wealthier people owned wells of good quality. Neither surface water nor well water was in short supply in this city built on lowlands, marshes, and alluvium. Not its shortage but the water quality varied a great deal from area to area within the town.

In the new system, water drawn from the Hooghly River was stored in settling tanks, filtered and restored in covered wells, and supplied to homes via pipes. The capacity was six million gallons a day. In a city of seven hundred thousand, the supply amounted to a meager per capita entitlement. The fact is much of the piped water went to a central district where the wealthiest residents lived.

Planning of space was not a strong point of the port city. Historians make much of the racial character of urban space in colonial cities: Europeans lived in white towns, Asians in black townships, and so on. The segregated nature is exaggerated and can be a misleading description. That the European and the Indian quarters were often demarcated in Calcutta, Madras, and Bombay had less to do with race than with wealth. People purchased land according to their financial capacity. The more prosperous the city, the more expensive land became. The cosmopolitan business elite lived in garden-encircled houses. The elite set had many Europeans in the early 1800s, but it was mainly Indian in all port cities by the end of the century. All employed many servants and owned wells and waste-disposal systems. These things needed ample space, and therefore a spacious garden house mattered to hygiene.

Beyond that core, there were old Indian settlers, Anglo-Indian populations, Indo-Portuguese people, and new migrants. The more recent the migrant, the more difficult it was to find a spacious place to live. Those engaged in wage work, in semiskilled or unskilled occupations, lived with little space and were pushed farther out to the suburbs. These localities were outside the municipal administration, to begin with. Houses there drew water from tanks and wells. As these areas grew bigger, they became centers of disease. Municipal limits extended to enfold some of these areas. In the race against population growth, some "suburban townships which encircle Calcutta" fell behind and "remained unreformed in respect of water supply."[14]

What was the water system like in these settlements? A description from Calcutta (1903) paints a picture:

Between the main thoroughfares are vast areas, with houses and huts built very closely and in an apparently inextricable confusion, crowded to the last degree with inhabitants. The floors are on the ground; there are no sewers, and the crooked ways between the houses simply reek with filth and moisture. Alongside of some of these paths, between three to four story buildings, are places that through the bars resemble dungeons in which many people live. There are numerous wells with water some 6 feet from the surface used by the natives, which readily account for the continuance of cholera.[15]

In 1903, piped water was a familiar system in the city's central districts, whereas in the suburbs "surface water from tanks, reservoirs, and wells" still supplied the bulk of the drinking water for the residents.[16] The description shows the persistence of a dualism well into the modern times.

In the peninsular regions and the interior, securing water for the cities was a harder challenge.

* * *

In the eighteenth century, the East India Company's primary business in India was procuring locally made cotton cloth from India for the European market. Of the three towns it set up, Madras retained the character of an artisanal town the longest. In the early 1800s, it had a European and Indo-European settlement developed around a fort and the garrison living in it, which was surrounded by villages. Some of these villages predated the company, but others had once produced and processed cloth for the firm. As the city grew, the density of the population in these "urban villages" increased. [17]

Water came from rivers, streams, and wells. Wealthier residents in the villages had their private wells, a pattern persisting into the twentieth century. For the others, water was getting scarcer and more deficient in quality as the population rose. The garrison got its water from seven wells constructed around 1772. "In former times," an 1867 report in the *British Medical Journal* said, the water from the seven wells "was regarded as very good, but [had] latterly been found overcharged with impurities."[18] Soldiers' health was a matter of concern, as said before. The 1867 report prepared the way for a piped and filtered water system constructed around 1872.

The water was available both for the Indo-European town and for the village-like settlements within the city limits.[19]

Madras's environment was different from that of Bombay and Calcutta in several ways. Unlike the other two cities, Madras relied mainly on the northeast monsoon. The average annual rainfall in the town is about half of Bombay's and 20 percent lower than Calcutta's. The average yearly temperature is also higher in the city. Because of the higher average temperature and more modest rainfall, surface water and groundwater in the town were subject to sharper variations. Tanks and wells were high-maintenance options.

The two main rivers flowing through the city are the Adyar and the Cooum. The Adyar flows for about twenty-seven miles from a western source. The Cooum originates in a tank about thirty-five miles to the west of the city. A five-mile-long canal, the Buckingham, constructed in 1877 as a famine relief project, links the two rivers near the sea. Within the city limits, the Cooum and the Buckingham became polluted channels in the late twentieth century because of sewage disposal. Further, all three watercourses were inundation channels carrying enough water in the monsoons. They were of little insurance value during droughts. Besides these rivers, there were several constructed lakes, or tanks, in or near the city. Water in the tanks suffered high evaporation. These features boiled down to one thing: waterworks in Madras were a more expensive proposition and, with smaller business incomes, imposed hardship on the town authority.

The larger of the cities in the interior revealed other forms of the technological challenge involved in securing water for a growing population.

* * *

Not far from Bombay, Ahmadabad had developed a sizable industrial base in the nineteenth century. In principle, funding waterworks should have been more accessible there with many wealthy potential taxpayers. Things were not so simple. By 1880, the town was home to many wealthy bankers and a few industrialists. The presence of wealthy merchants and a powerful state did not translate into efficient civic management. As in Bombay, the attempt to use wealth and power to improve public health often generated fierce quarrels. Merchants were reluctant to fund public projects, and the imperial administration was more interested in trade growth.

Leadership made a difference. The start of piped water in Ahmadabad is linked to the name of the pioneer industrialist of the city, Ranchhodlal Chhotalal (1823–1898). Even by the standards of self-made men, Chhotalal was quite extraordinary. He came from a traditional Brahmin family of Gujarat, equipped himself for an administrative career by learning English, traveled widely, and befriended British military officers and merchants. These offbeat associations led to the decision to set up the first cotton textile mill of Ahmadabad town, for which he campaigned with Baroda bankers and princely states and, not so successfully, with the trading classes. By 1870, when he was a wealthy industrialist, Chhotalal joined a campaign for water supply and underground drainage schemes in the town. His worry was cholera. The disease broke out often and took a heavy toll on the cotton mill workers' settlements.

As earlier in his life, he faced opposition from the merchants who already owned wells. The European and Parsi engineer corps disagreed in their view of the merits of these schemes. Chhotalal insisted and almost got beaten up in a public meeting. His extensive political connection, personal wealth, and goodwill with the British administration saw these schemes through.[20]

* * *

Bombay's impounding reservoir system had a counterpart in the Deccan cities, especially Hyderabad, where large constructed lakes trapped rainwater for use in the drier seasons. In Pune, a somewhat similar system was followed. The drier the region, the more limited the capacity of the mechanism.

For centuries since its foundation in 1591, Hyderabad drew water from human-made lakes trapping rainwater and wells. Between 1920 and 1927, lakes of much larger capacity than those in existence were created by first damming two minor rivers, both tributaries of the Krishna, and then damming the Manjira, a tributary of the Godavari. The Krishna basin projects supplied water to the city, and the Godavari basin projects provided water to farmlands over a wider region. Soon after independence, the Godavari basin water was trapped in several new dams. Hyderabad's water problems were temporarily solved to begin again in the late twentieth century.[21]

After independence from colonial rule, and reorganization of state boundaries that soon followed, the two main river basins of the Deccan spanned several states that wanted the water generated from it. Ideally, river basin management should be under one authority, but such a body was impractical because the rivers passed through several states. In the late twentieth century, the population began to grow fast within the city and suburbs. Intensive agriculture made more substantial drafts on the water available from the old river basin projects. The river basins fell short of the needs. Hyderabad could get water via reallocation from agricultural uses.

Like other towns in the Deccan, Pune residents drew their water from wells until the 1870s and from aqueducts constructed in the eighteenth century to bring into the town water from tanks located in the Katraj valley. Other minor aqueducts followed, delivering water from springs and wells nearby. Nothing much happened in the early nineteenth century because of political uncertainty in the region. After the British takeover in 1818, the town remained dormant for several decades, emerging again as an economic hub after railway connection with Bombay opened in 1869. In 1856, a town municipality had come into existence. After the 1876–1878 drought, the Mutha River was dammed to create the Kharakwasla reservoir. Much of the public water supply then came from Katraj and Kharakwasla via aqueducts.[22] In the twentieth century, these aqueducts deposited the water in tanks, where coagulation and filtration treatments were added before the water flowed out into taps.

Between 1878 and 1936, water available from public taps in Pune increased from 15 gallons (per head per day) to 55 gallons, and the number of connections increased almost ninefold, from 1,150 in 1884 to more than 9,000.[23] An impressive growth, it was bought at a hefty price. The waterworks were the most significant public utilities maintained by the town authority. Construction and maintenance were expensive, and the revenue was insufficient. A 1923 expansion of the system (necessitated by the shift to flushing toilets from the manual collection of night soil) was paid for by a public loan and a government grant. A tight capital market depressed investment, as it did in Madras too. It was only after 1947 that a fresh burst of investment began.

More or less using local tanks and rivers, most towns in southern India developed their own piped water system in the early twentieth century. In 1930, a report on Hyderabad stated, every district headquarter town had piped water supply.[24] Like Hyderabad and Pune, Bangalore relied on reservoirs constructed on local rivers. One of these was built in 1894 on the Arkavathy, a tributary of the Kaveri River, and another was created in 1933 (the Hesarghatta and the Tippagondanahalli).

There was a pattern to these stories. Between 1858 and 1880, three things had emerged, enabling a common technological-institutional framework for water supply to appear in the cities. These were large engineering projects using stored or dammed water, the creation of a municipal authority and a tax center, and a company that owned the filtration and coagulation lakes and arranged for connection to piped water. From that origin, the water supply in the towns tried to keep in step with population growth. The port cities had a faster population growth rate. More water set off a race between infrastructure and in-migration. The infrastructure needed to grow fast and find the money to construct extensions. There was more money in these cities, but the moneyed did not always want to pay for public goods. The technological principle did not change much either, not at least until the late twentieth century. Despite the infrastructure, then, water distribution inside the city was often insufficient, skewed, and reliant on private sources.

The story gets more complicated when we factor in location and size. In towns of larger size, like the three port cities, the framework operated on a larger scale. In smaller towns, it was less developed relative to the needs. Further, in dry southern and interior western India (Hyderabad, Pune, Bangalore, and to some extent Madras), construction of waterworks was more expensive because the local water sources did not carry enough. In the end, the works delivered limited output. The reliance on wells and the maldistribution were both more acute in these cities for a long time.

When India became independent from colonial rule, the inequality between small and large towns and the village and the city was wide.

* * *

India's Environmental Hygiene Committee in 1949 estimated that 49 percent of the urban population had piped and cleaned water supply in some form. Depending on population density, "the supplies were designed to give 2 to 40 gallons per head per day." The situation in the villages "could not be assessed by the Committee even approximately."[25] Although the two five-year plans (1951–1955 and 1956–1960) allocated a sum of money for water supply schemes, progress in the villages was slow. A national water supply and sanitation program could not cover more than fifteen thousand villages, or a little over 2 percent of the total number. In the rest, conditions were too different from state to state, village to village, and season to season.

We can do better with the numbers. We know that in 1951, the Indian Union had a rural population of 299 million and an urban population of 61 million. Setting average urban consumption at 20 gallons per day per head (the midpoint of the Environmental Hygiene Committee's range), and taking a total water consumption of 11 billion cubic meters (based on table 1.1), these figures give us a rural use of 18 gallons per head per day. For every 10 percent increase in average urban consumption, rural consumption fell by 1.5 gallons per head per day. These numbers are *low* and suggest wide inequality.

How low? How unequal? In 1950, an average American consumed 145 gallons per day.[26] An average Briton consumed a slightly smaller quantity. All of India consumed a fraction of what the inhabitants of the United States and Europe did. Cities like Bombay, Calcutta, Madras, and Pune had daily water use of around 50 gallons per head.[27] The bigger cities in India were far more water-secure than smaller towns, and towns a lot more secure than the countryside. But even the most water-secure in India would look severely deprived compared with the Europeans and the Americans.

The countryside posed a many-sided challenge. After independence, when money was allocated to the rural water supply, a lot of it remained unspent in 1960. Money spent on a large scheme served larger numbers and could expect to collect taxes—only in a city, not in the villages. Even when water was a pure public good and left to government departments, new problems arose. In most states, there was bureaucratic discord, a late colonial legacy made more complicated by the proliferation of new offices. Unlike with urban water supply, "a number of agencies [were] in charge of rural water supply" schemes.[28] The district administration, the public health engineers, the tribal welfare agency, all had a say in how money should be spent.

The old combination of private and public investment continued into the decades of the mid-twentieth century. The balance between these two modes of supply changed in favor of municipal water, sometimes to the detriment of the users. For example, a 1947 report found that many old wells in Madras city and the province had been neglected because people had come to depend on municipal taps. And yet, municipalities had not grown in capacity in step with the population. In a few cases, individual houses in the localities had access to municipal water taps, but "in many instances there [was] a single tap for the whole village." "The women feel it a great hardship to have to walk five minutes from their door to the tap and five minutes back in order to get a pot full of water, there are often struggles for first place at the tap and many have to wait for a very long time for their turn."[29] This description of the 1920s has a timeless relevance.

There were other significant changes to add to the challenge of meeting urban demand. The balance between the seaboard and the interior changed after 1947. Independent India's development policy placed a heavy accent on producing metals, machines, and chemicals. Some of the earlier businesses—commodity trade, foreign trade, and traditional industry like the textiles—declined. The seaboard cities retreated in economic importance. The major cities, Bombay and Calcutta, experienced an extended period of urban unrest and deindustrialization in the 1970s and the 1980s.

By contrast, the rates of public saving and public investment increased. They concentrated on heavy industrial plants set up by the government in the interior cities. A lot of the subsidies also went into the provision of agricultural inputs, fertilizers, seeds, and electric power to raise water. While Bombay and Calcutta retreated, interior cities like Bangalore and Bhopal forged ahead based on heavy doses of public investment in industrial development. Private and government efforts to mobilize water also increased as part of these policies. In a general sense, there was a convergence between the interior urban space and the seaboard city as a result. Still, the interior was more water-scarce and not the best choice for building large cities.

It is a paradox, then, that a recent economic resurgence would concentrate in the interior cities.

* * *

The economic boom India experienced starting in the late 1980s was an urban phenomenon. By the 1990s, when India liberalized its highly regulated economy, the green revolution (1965–1985) was past its peak, and the countryside was under economic pressure. The reforms saved the situation by creating jobs in urban-based service industries. Indeed, the boom was a big-city phenomenon. Like Bangalore or Madras, some of these cities emerged as global service export hubs and magnets to a skilled and educated workforce. From 18 percent in 1951, the urban ratio rose to exceed 30 percent in 2010.

As the population density in the inner areas increased and apartment blocks took over space, the old-style homestead wells started to disappear. But municipal water was continually falling behind demand. In the apartments as well as the homesteads, bore wells took over. The municipal tap developed an association with the poorer residents of the city. A history of bore wells in postcolonial India suggests that in discourses in policy and planning circles, private investment and the tube well received stress from the 1950s on.[30] But the mode of investment did not change radically. It remained statist. The late twentieth century saw explosive growth in private investment.

Large numbers of people from the countryside came to the cities to work in manufacturing, construction, and semi-skilled services. The economic boom was unplanned and simply allowed to happen. The cities where it unfolded had no time to prepare for the expansion of the workforce. The city authorities permitted settlements to grow on common lands, lowlands, or derelict water bodies. Or new plans encompassed villages into the city's territory, weakening local systems of managing common property without offering a better alternative. Too often, a land mafia became involved in converting common property such as dry tank beds or pastures to dwellings.

Because of the chaos of economic emergence, income poverty was not always the reason for water poverty in the big city. Nor was underinvestment in infrastructure or limited tax collection the reason. Residents in municipality-administered land had access to shared faucets and more of them. Still, 60 percent or more of urban slums in India were "non-notified" around 2015, neither administered nor recognized by the city authority. These places had neither a secure water supply nor an adequate sewage and waste disposal system. On average, about half the people living in urban areas had supplies of water within their homes. Most lived on common and unsafe water.[31] Most people who lived in these areas would access water, even municipal water, by negotiating with a variety of suppliers. These "multiple water regimes," as one study of Bombay (now Mumbai) called them, remained beyond regulatory reach but were part of the everyday reality of those who lived in these slums (figure 5.1).[32]

Not all cities are as well served by nature as Bombay. In dry areas, shortages were brutal and improvised strategies more difficult to rely on. The governments seemed to be caught in a bind. To provide essential services to these areas amounted to accepting the encroachment on common lands

Figure 5.1 Water tanker in a suburb. Most towns and cities drew water from a nearby secure source. But rising population made the source inadequate from time to time. From times past, water markets and traveling storage, distinctly urban systems, helped lessen the impact of temporary scarcities. This picture from the outskirts of Bhiwandi near Mumbai shows a water tanker, and a thirsty girl taking a quick drink before the water is distributed away. Credit: Akella Srinivas Ramalingaswami and Shutterstock.

or government-owned lands these settlements started from. To not offer essential services invited the charge that the indifference was "in violation of its obligations to progressively realize the human right to water and sanitation under international human rights law, as well as its obligations under the right to life provisions of the Indian constitution."[33]

At the same time, a new kind of community was forming in the city, a "middle-class community," a network of people who shared a worry. The worry was, left to the government, urban commons would be lost forever. Although many of Bangalore's old tanks were in bad shape through urban growth, some became the center of conservationist activism.[34]

The drive behind water infrastructure in the cities thus changed. In one view, the old public health and public good drives gave way to a fuller play of private capital and commercial considerations in urban infrastructural development.[35] The same tendency generated a reaction. A work on Madras (now Chennai) suggests that the authorities running large cities began to experience an "ecological enlightenment" from around 2000, when an older tendency to resettle populations on derelict water bodies gave way to a tendency to reclaim, revive, and beautify water bodies, often by resettling slums situated on them.[36] The shift was owed in part to a realization that the attrition of water bodies in the past wrecked drainage enough to cause monsoon floods.

* * *

"As India urbanises," writes a contemporary survey on water, "the growing proportions of its population [will] come into contact with formal water service providers."[37] Such expectation implies reduced barriers to access. But "formal service providers" have not always been there in the city from the start. Chapter 5 has shown the emergence of public water supply, its impact on access and living standards, and why the model fell behind in the late twentieth century. As it fell behind, deprivation and groundwater exploitation rose.

Both chapter 4 on irrigation and chapter 5 on the cities end uneasily with a scenario of competition and conflict. Chapter 6 is all about competition and conflict.

6

WATER STRESS

Frequent disputes regarding river waters [make] just solutions difficult.
—Justice V. B. Eradi, Ravi and Beas Waters Tribunal, 1987

Thousands of Bengali farmers and their families migrated from East Pakistan in the aftermath of the Partition of India in 1947. Land was short in densely populated West Bengal. The government offered a deal, one that rulers in the past often used: develop rugged land, and it is yours for free. There was plenty of land in the great Indian plateau, and several thousand Bengalis were taken there. What they found was an environment where land was of little value, water was difficult to store, and their farming knowledge that took abundant surface water for granted was useless. Politicians rushed to close their choice. In a parliamentary debate on the fiasco, a legislator complained of the ungrateful settlers: "They said 'We want . . . the big rivers of East Bengal.' [They should have realized that nobody would come forward to] create rivers for them."[1] This episode was one of the rarer cases of sharing an ecological space between dissimilar communities. Since the 1950s, many more cases would occur on sharing water, and few of these ended in an agreement.

Big schemes increasing supplies were no solution. In parallel, two technological responses to water shortage became shaky in the twentieth century. Impounding excess flow in rivers via dams and reservoirs seemed like an obvious idea in a monsoon climate with a vast "wastage" of rainwater. In the 1920s, however, some began to think that intensive cultivation and the river projects were changing local environments for the worse. After 1947, the criticisms drowned under the excitement over national development, and India built numerous projects on the principle. After the 1970s, however, the model was as good as abandoned for the high environmental and political costs it entailed. Individuals and businesses moved to explore groundwater. The second model risked the exhaustion of shallow aquifers. A great deal of the current scholarship on water in India is a response to the prospect.

But now the public trust doctrine was in place. There was more data on the capacity of aquifers. Many nongovernmental organizations (NGOs) became involved in the conservation effort. Do these changes amount to a significant shift? How big is the shift?

Chapter 6 describes the journey from one paradigm to another. A useful point to start is an early discourse on the environmental damage caused by agricultural expansion.

* * *

The colonial preoccupation with rivers sometimes led to a neglect of traditional resource management systems like tanks.[2] In late colonial India, a few officers criticized the cost of mass irrigation. The irrigation canals taken from the Himalayan rivers sometimes degraded soil or risked hazards like malaria.[3] In the western part of the Indo-Gangetic basin, where subsoil water was used for cultivation, groundwater reservoirs were at risk. In some tracts, the uncertainty raised the cost of constructing a new well and of extraction of water.[4] A similar process occurred in a few dry areas that had experienced agricultural intensification.[5]

In the eastern part of the basin and the Bengal delta, which relied on the deltaic and rain-fed rivers for subsistence and winter cultivation, a change in the morphology of the river system had set in. Deltaic Bengal became fertile and retained fertility through a natural process, a change in the course of the rivers. In the monsoons, numerous small channels carried excess river water into depressions, turning them into tanks. As the tanks drained again, the dried-up tank beds provided fields for rabi (winter-sown) crops. In western Bengal, overexpansion of cultivation since the nineteenth century had started to restrain the process, with the result that the soil surrounding the rivers deteriorated.[6]

An example of the crisis was the Damodar River, which degenerated into a narrow and fixed channel on reaching lower Bengal. In eastern Bengal, many agricultural tracts were said to be "dying." The reason was that the tanks neither had enough water nor dried in time.[7] The problem appeared because of the silting up of the rivers and of the channels carrying excess river water. These became swamps in the dry season and breeding grounds for mosquitoes carrying malaria.

Canal irrigation did not invite much criticism in the colonial period. Indeed, it gained in popularity. In the interwar period, dams and canals would serve other purposes such as electricity generation. The large-scale systems were the so-called multipurpose projects constructed over rivers to create a reservoir, a hydroelectric power generation plant, and irrigation by canals. In the 1950s, a new strategy focused on building dams in the western rivers flowing through undulated terrain. In eastern India, the dam had another use, flood control by trapping monsoon water. Because of soil and topography, most Bengal rivers carried an enormous quantity of silt. During heavy monsoons, floods were inevitable. Premodern and colonial states spent much energy building embankments, where a river flowed through a flat terrain. For forty years after India's independence, occasional evidence of the declining quality of surface water did not trouble the policy makers too much. Nor was there a radical shift in the paradigm of hydraulic engineering. Hundreds of dams got built to serve irrigation, electricity, and flood control.

By the 1970s, the costs of the strategy were becoming too great to ignore. The dams built over a twenty-five-to-thirty-year period since 1950—temples of modern India, as India's first prime minister, Jawaharlal Nehru, called them—caused floods because the reservoirs were overfull during monsoons and forced the engineers to release excess water at short notice. They degraded land by interfering with natural silt flows; interfered with aquatic life; destroyed forests; caused waterlogging, salination, and diseases; displaced people; and increased earthquake risk.[8] Several reservoirs attached to the dams silted fast; the silting happened on such a large scale as to make dredging impossible (figure 6.1).

Canals came under attack too. Canals encouraged wastage at the head reach and caused shortage at the tail end.[9] Farmers adapted cropping patterns to seasonal scarcity and devised their own rules to contain open conflicts.[10] But these methods operated locally. There were high transmission losses in the conveyance from the source to points of use, a syndrome called low levels of water productivity.[11] An

WATER STRESS

Figure 6.1 The Hirakud Dam. In rain-fed rivers throughout India, enormous reservoirs were built after 1947 to help agriculture, flood control, and drinking waters shortages. The Hirakud Dam, built on the Mahanadi, was one of these projects. Since the 1980s, industrialization, mining, effluents release, and paddy cultivation took a heavy toll on the reservoir and the quality of its water. Before the dam existed, Hirakud was an island in the river. The island was once known for diamond mining; the word *hira* means "diamonds." Credit: Bikash Padhee and Shutterstock.

apparent reason for high losses was evaporation, but management and engineering failure compounded the problem. Carelessly lined canals caused a lot of water to percolate underground.[12]

In the 1990s, the campaign against big dams reached a peak during protests about the Narmada River project. The project was conceived in the 1950s. Serious construction work started in the 1980s. When it was apparent that the project would have extensive displacement and environmental consequences, a few Indian NGOs campaigned against the project. International NGOs rallied to the campaign and forced one of the major funders of the project, the World Bank, to reassess its involvement.[13] The project did go forward, but against fierce criticism, and was possibly the last multipurpose river basin project to materialize in India.

Throughout, the critics targeted the displacement issue more energetically than the effects on the environment. The Narmada episode showed that there was no easy way to manage the displacement of people, and with rising population density, the problem would only get messier. With all the side effects, impounding monsoon water may still be the best technical solution to water problems, and still the most obvious one, but the human costs of large-scale projects rose because matching institutional response did not happen.

Another issue was becoming politically intractable, disputes over water, between countries and provinces (discussed below) and between types of user. With canals, head-reach and tail-end farmers faced different levels of water security, as noted before. Several Deccan plateau projects just did not deliver enough water, and the farmers, thus deprived, refused to pay taxes. In 1979–1980, a movement formed in Navalgund, in Karnataka state, to protest taxes for water collected from a river valley project. The tax, it was said, did not discriminate between the two sets of users. The inequality, if not redressed by collective action or state intervention, would induce one group of farmers to overuse water and switch to water-intensive crops and another group to seek alternative sources and other livelihoods.[14]

The sharing of river flows between the nation-states of South Asia was always tense, and became more so.

* * *

Three large economies in South Asia share the Indo-Gangetic basin water. India and Pakistan rely on the five rivers of the Indus basin for irrigation and power. All these rivers originate inside India, and four of them flow inside Pakistan. The Indus Waters Treaty of 1960 allowed Pakistan to exploit the western rivers more while granting India rights to the eastern rivers. The treaty survived relatively trouble-free until 2002. After that, threatening words were exchanged on several occasions.

Hydropolitical analysis has grown alarmist. South Asia contains over a fifth of the world's population and has 8 percent of the global freshwater. Most sources of freshwater the South Asian countries share, and India shares with China. The prospect of going to war over water is not beyond imagination.[15] As of now, the nations of South Asia are cooperating more than disputing their rights to riparian resources. The terms of negotiation, critics believe, reflect the economic weight of the countries more than ecological considerations.[16] And the prospect of climate change shifts the geographical knowledge base on which some of the treaties were drawn.[17]

In Pakistan, "the potential for political instability over domestic water distribution and development" became increasingly real.[18] A study of the Indus basin shows that these conflicts did not directly stem from absolute scarcity; rather, they were entangled in the discourses on entitlement to water. They related to broader political processes such as "democratization, . . . social justice, [articulation of] ethnic, religious, and linguistic identity," and perceptions of groups of claimants about justice and economic security.[19] The simple shortage does not explain the emerging conflicts at the local levels. These conflicts embedded in beliefs that water was a democratic and human right, which some stakeholders violated at the cost of others.

If international disputes were tense, interstate disputes over rivers tested the federal state's institutions.

* * *

At the end of the eighteenth century, the ruler of Hyderabad gifted a large tract of land to the East India Company in exchange for military protection. The area, known as the Ceded Districts in the colonial sources, was one of the driest parts of South India. The Deccan famines had affected it, and the memory lived long. Consisting of the Anantapur, Cuddapah, Kurnool, Chittoor, Adoni, and Bellary Districts, the area became known as Rayalaseema in the late colonial period. A regional movement emerged on the back of a strong sense of economic deprivation relative to the other areas of the Madras Presidency. Insecurity over water was the critical measure of deprivation.[20] The movement prepared the ground for creating a unified Andhra Pradesh state, on condition that Rayalaseema would get river-water-sharing deals to compensate for its disadvantage. A series of river projects using the waters of the Tungabhadra and its tributaries took shape after independence.

Rayalaseema was not the only region to harbor similar feelings. A similar process occurred in the Deccan at large, where five states shared three river basins of limited capacity and fluctuating levels of supply. Interstate disputes over river water involve two or more territorial units at different reaches of a river. In 1956, the Interstate River Water Disputes Act created a framework for negotiation, inquiries, tribunals, and an appeals process, where states shared rivers. The act took over the task earlier performed by state-appointed tribunals, as in the Kaveri waters dispute.

The history of agreements to share the Kaveri waters goes back to the early twentieth-century treaties between the princely state of Mysore and the British-ruled Madras

Presidency. A larger share of the waters went to the agriculturally developed deltaic Tamil Nadu region, whereas a larger share of the basin fell in the Karnataka region. The waters sustained intensive cultivation in the Thanjavur rice belt. The agreements set limits on intra-territory usage and dam building and reservoir capacity in the river's upper reaches. From the 1970s on, the green revolution, industrialization, and urban demand increased water usage throughout the basin. After 1990, the tribunal process turned disputatious. On two occasions, 1995 and 2002, a bad monsoon reduced water flow in the river and the reservoirs and compelled Karnataka to capture a larger share than before, causing a mass protest in Tamil Nadu. Although a river authority now oversaw the sharing arrangements, the dispute moved to the Supreme Court.

What does the dispute tell us? The Kaveri is a rain-fed river, and its flow depends on the strength of the monsoon. Every new bad rainy season created more intense desperation and anxiety, and the dispute erupted with greater force. Further, the normal fluctuation in the flow level made it harder to calculate what water was utilizable, leaving all allocations open to disputation. Above all, there was a growing mismatch between demand and supply. Long-term supply conditions had not changed much, but demand had risen a lot because the population had grown, and the states with stakes in the waters of the river were at the forefront of the economic emergence process. Following a long-held tradition, dispute resolution focused on the river rather than on managing demand.

Another dispute in northern India did generate a discussion on demand management. Three northern states, Punjab, Haryana, and Rajasthan (and Pakistan) share the waters of the Ravi and the Beas. The history of intensive agriculture there went back to colonial times. In 1966, the Haryana state separated from Punjab, and river sharing now came under the interstate negotiations system. The river-sharing arrangement had given more water to Punjab. The deals came under strain after the 1970s green revolution increased water usage. Usage exploded after rice cultivation grew in a later green revolution. As in the Kaveri, tribunals, political agreements, and court judgments tried to resolve the problem. And as in the Kaveri, the growing mismatch between supply and demand, as agriculture and the cities made an ever-rising draft on the available waters, made resolution hard to achieve. The statement by V. B. Eradi, a judge in the Supreme Court and the head of one of the Ravi and Beas tribunals, cited at the beginning of the chapter, reflects this impasse. When the dispute revived in the late 1980s, a book published on water sharing in the Ravi-Beas basins reviewed the supply conditions with a lot of new data and then commented on the prospects of economizing.[21] One conclusion stood out. Paddy cultivation was a bad idea in water-scarce regions. Even when sprinkler-type technology was used for other crops, it did not work in rice fields.

The most recent interstate dispute broke out between Chhattisgarh and Odisha states over the water of the Mahanadi River. It had features in common with other interstate disputes: a sharp rise in demand (from industry), an initially unequal sharing arrangement, the conflict between users in the upper and the lower reaches, and divergence between federal and state politics.[22]

Compared with rivers, underground water was a conflict-free option, or so it seemed.

* * *

The provincial governments in the dry areas knew the value of wells. A near famine in Rayalaseema in the 1950s drew soldiers into action, as they took over wells, built new ones, and deepened the existing ones. Around 1951–1952, the government of Rajasthan had in its employment a "water diviner." The water diviner stayed in one place for a few days to activate a sort of sixth sense, which determined whether there was underground water there or not. Geologists protested that the state wasted its money on a superstition. Uncannily, a geologist and the diviner often zeroed in on the same spots. The community development projects built many wells, some with the diviner's help.

That the farmers in canal areas valued wells more than canals became obvious a little later as the green revolution unfolded. In 1971, there was a symposium on water resources.[23] The papers read there said that the paradigm of irrigation the state had so far relied on, the multipurpose river basin projects, was not the preferred option of the farmers. Farmers who hoped to gain from the high-yielding seed-fertilizer combination invested in wells. They did because they wanted to control water application better, whereas canal water flooded the land. By 1990, the canal model was as good as dead, thanks to the political costs, and private investment in tube wells had taken over as the paradigm of water sourcing in the farms. The shift involved a significant rise in the energy intensity of irrigation. Dug wells dominated the wells scene until 1980; in the next thirty years, their proportion came down to about a third of all wells. The rest were newly built deep or shallow tube wells run with electric power.

In 1997, the Punjab government announced that farmers would get electricity for free. The groundwater level in the state started to drop soon after the announcement. By 2013, the groundwater level had fallen from five meters below ground level to about fifteen meters below ground level.[24] The extraordinary growth in wells causing the sharp drop did not just come from a subsidy. There was a geographical dimension to the growth. The hard rock aquifers of the Deccan Traps are quite expensive to exploit. Wells are cheaper to build, and the aquifers larger in the north. "In an alluvial aquifer system," therefore, "the impact of an individual user's extraction on the aquifer as a whole is limited. Hence, there is a great incentive to collude and collectively exploit the aquifer."[25]

Whether there was a causal link between the announcement and the decline in groundwater level is open to debate. More states followed the Punjab example in offering free or flat rate power, and a perception grew that free power to farmers was a political necessity. The fear was misplaced. Some states did break the rule without significant cost to the party leading the reform.[26] In any case, the groundwater crisis appeared in the same period in many states (figure 6.2).

A reason the crisis appeared when it did is that bore wells and urbanization have become interdependent in recent times. Eighty percent of urban and industrial water now comes from wells. In a tropical monsoon land, the ratio is not good news for groundwater management.

* * *

Cities in India rose or fell based on the health of the local water sources. Medieval towns like Fatehpur Sikri near Agra or Gaur (Gauda) and Saptagram in Bengal were abandoned because rechargeable water sources ran out. Thanks to the low cost of water extraction from a nearby source, urban growth led to an overreliance on a fixed source and to crises

WATER STRESS 125

Figure 6.2 Drought in Marathwada. Marathwada, covering much of the southeastern section of the Deccan Traps (figure 1.2), is vulnerable to droughts. When one breaks out, technology fails, and water must be rationed, causing long lines like the one shown. Credit: Dinodia Photo.

and depopulation. Such dynamics have been typical in other world regions too. Cycles of growth–overuse–abandonment became rarer (or perhaps more long-drawn-out) starting in the nineteenth century because of the impounding and storage projects that served the cities (chapter 5).

Threatened by overuse, the city continually looked beyond its borders. Since the 1990s, water conflict grew in India's megacities, where "a combination of institutional path dependence and a neo-liberal restructuring" had "extended the ability of [the cities] to establish new forms of water entitlement in rural and peri-urban areas."[27] Water allocation to the cities involved stormy negotiations between the municipality and the farmers around the city. On several occasions, these started as discussions between the ministries in charge of drinking water and irrigation. Almost invariably, the talks failed, farmers protested, the highest level of political authority in the state got involved in the process, and tribunals and courts resolved the dispute with an order, which was soon outdated. The more publicized of such disputes involved Hyderabad, Pune, Mumbai (Bombay), and Bangalore.

Allocating water between farmers and city dwellers involves a trade-off. Farmers who are poorer than the city residents complain of deprivation. And yet, in the presence of subsidization of irrigation, only the urban water supply is financially self-sustainable. Scholars suggest two ways to achieve responsible use of the commons, sale and appropriation.[28] Economists explore market-based solutions such as the purchase of water. Geographers and political scientists observe that nonmarket processes, often called capture and appropriation, prevail in many cases. Few such appropriation cases involve extralegal or coercive means. More often, political arm-twisting addresses the issues.

These conflicts appear when a state tries to allocate surface water between farmers who carry votes and city dwellers who command wealth. Conflicts disappear when both are permitted to draw water from underground. Groundwater took over because it was politically the happiest medium. In 1876, the private well in a famine zone was a symbol of inequality between the rich and the poor. In 2000, wells served both the "poor" farmers and the rich city dwellers. Both belonged to powerful lobbies. As for the farmers, it was the fortunate access to canal water that symbolized inequality. "Groundwater," by contrast, was the "'democratic resource' taking the benefit of irrigation to every corner . . . and the mainstay of small and marginal farmers eking out a living from their shrinking holdings by working their land more intensively."[29] Provincial politics would defend the rights of the small farmers to extract water from the underground because big votes were at stake there. The apartment dwellers in the cities also lived on their own bore wells. Who would question these elites who spearheaded India's economic emergence? With the poor and the rich making a common cause, politics was powerless to challenge extraction of groundwater. Private investment was efficient, democratic, but draining.

By the late twentieth century, the claims on subsoil water exploded. Economic growth in India since the 1990s created the fear that nonagricultural demand for water was growing too fast.

* * *

The worry came from the evidence of overuse of the aquifers. India's second and rice-based green revolution of the 1980s was a success of food production at an enormous environmental cost. Soil nutrients depleted in many cases, and groundwater was mined recklessly. Between 1995 and 2004, the proportion of the Indian population living in "unsafe" districts—unsafe being defined as the aquifers' declining capacity to recharge and sustain current levels of water extraction—increased from 7 to 35 percent.[30] In the northern districts leading the earlier wheat-based green revolution, exploitation of groundwater in the 1990s reached levels that far exceeded the capacity of the aquifers to sustain. Pakistan faced the problem on a bigger scale. Elsewhere, the hydrogeological conditions influencing supply varied too much to make predictions on future supply a simple matter. However, the main issue was not the quantum of potential supply; it was that groundwater appeared as a private good to the users, whereas it came from a common pool.

Groundwater use also raised concerns about inequality and water quality. Wells are a private investment. Although sometimes well construction is subsidized, on average, the rich have a greater capacity to make private investment than the poor, whether in the countryside for agriculture or in the cities for drinking or industrial purposes. Wells, therefore, generate inequality and are not the democratic option they are often touted as.

Since the 1990s, private well construction for both urban and rural use has progressed at a faster pace than public supplies of water.[31] Practically, there was a retreat from the principle that underground aquifers belonged to everyone. Water became private again. Caste and status as a ticket to access water in the cities did not work anymore. Wealth and profession were better predictors of security of access. Overuse of groundwater caused a fall in the quality of water. In the Krishna River basin, overexploitation caused reduction as well as salinization of the upper aquifers.[32] In West Bengal and Bangladesh, tube-well water contains dangerous levels of arsenic; whether due to natural properties of the soil or to overuse of chemical fertilizers is not known.

What could be done?

* * *

The possibility of a causal link between policy and overuse underlined two messages animating recent discussions on water in India. First, there is scope for reform in policy to curtail use. And second, water use in agriculture must be curtailed anyhow without affecting crop production. If use can be trimmed without reducing production, then we say the productivity of water has increased.

It is a canon in the huge literature on common property resources that there are institutional solutions to the tragedy of the commons. There are three types of institutional solutions. These are state regulation and rationing, allowing markets a fuller play when resources can be priced, and cooperative rules of sharing. The late twentieth-century Indian experience with depletion of water does not inspire confidence in any of these solutions. The state has intervened in river water disputes. Such intervention contained the dispute but did not end it. Every drought rekindled the dispute, forcing the arbitration to start from scratch. Water markets require specific conditions to work at all and sometimes generated inequality. Cooperation again was a limited tool. The problem is not that Indians cannot cooperate (though caste does sometimes complicate matters) but that there is desperate water scarcity for all.

Since the 1990s, studies have shown that markets were more likely to emerge in commercial agriculture, producing a profitable crop. They appeared after the green revolution and rarely had older antecedents.[33] They were not part of a farming tradition or community tradition. Water markets also functioned better when the traders were from similar caste backgrounds. Too much diversity was bad for water trade, for "water transactions are strongly interpersonal," and "individuals tend to conduct such trade with members of their own caste or close relatives."[34] Market failure, which was "as endemic in irrigation and water management as government failure," did not just stem from the need to rely on personal ties.[35] Wells entailed a precarious private property right because the water underground could not be allocated. Someone with a bigger and deeper well could draw on the same water as a smaller well belonging to a poor farmer. There was no legal way to make the former pay more or pay compensation.

Further, water markets worked better in alluvial aquifers (as in Gujarat), where the capacity of pumps to extract water was relatively high, or well yields were high. "The situation is fundamentally different in hard rock areas where well yields are low and often vary greatly across seasons. In this situation, surpluses are far smaller and tend to vary across seasons and locations. It is a seller's market in which the bargaining position of water buyers is weak."[36]

If markets were an unreliable solution, did cooperation work better? Since the 1990s, or even before, NGOs have involved themselves in water conservation. Some of them did outstanding work. They advocated small-scale projects run by some kind of participatory setup. In such contexts, their involvement became relevant or even possible. Economic assessments of cooperative water management did not hold out a hopeful picture, however. Cooperatives required specific conditions to work at all. NGOs were exposed to the ups and downs of local politics, and not all parties trusted them.

Some necessary projects were too big. And private investment served some environments better.

In the Krishna River basin in the Deccan, water cooperatives existed (and still do). They required a profitable crop regime and interlocked transactions between land and water.[37] When sufficient water is available, richer farmers lease in land from poorer farmers to grow water-intensive and profitable crops, like sugarcane. . "Small or marginal farmers also get a share of 25 percent by leasing out their land, which is usually higher than what they would have got by growing subsistence crops."[38] Another cooperation model was to build around a small irrigation project, like a dam on a village channel or a lake to impound excess monsoon water, and then share the water within a local community. The model, first tried in a village near Pune city after a drought in 1972–1973, became famous as the *pani panchayat*, or water council.[39] It was later replicated in other states, such as Orissa (now Odisha), where the idea had the backing of specific legislation. The assessment of the scheme was mixed. In many instances, cooperation failed or produced limited benefits. Water councils exist in a small number of villages in rain-fed India.

An obvious obstacle to cooperation is inequality in landholding. If a few people in the village hold most irrigated land, they could influence the council. When the rich and the poor farmers belonged in different castes, the conflict took on a caste angle. Caste contributed to the "democratic deficit" that could bring councils down. At the least, caste reinforced economic inequality. "Lands in advantageous positions [to access surface water] are owned by the upper castes and communities. The access to groundwater resources also shows the same tendencies as those observed in the case of surface water."[40]

Despite the obvious problems, cooperative responses to irrigation water shortage around a micro-project have taken shape throughout the Deccan plateau and beyond. It is an attractive idea to those who suffer from droughts in a geographical setting where large river basin projects cannot work. What is micro-irrigation?

* * *

"There is a rich historical tradition of local water harvesting in India from the *ahar-pyne* system in Bihar, the *tankas* of Rajasthan, the Himalayan *dharas*, the *talabs* in Bundelkhand to the *eries* of Tamil Nadu."[41] Since the 1990s, amid a rethinking on water policy in India, stress fell on the restoration of these systems where they had fallen into disuse and the creation of similar systems where these did not exist. The impetus came from a new interest in watershed management in those states of India (mainly Maharashtra and Madhya Pradesh) where agriculture was still primarily rain-fed. A watershed is a system of small- and medium-scale works to control the natural flow of water in a small area (about twenty square miles). The strategy received funding support from federal and state governments and drew in many NGOs to work as consultants. While the benefits in soil conservation are clearer, how effective watershed management systems are in protecting dry-season water supply remains uncertain. The effect on irrigation water is small.

South India's tanks, or small water bodies as the World Bank calls them, irrigated a substantial percentage of croplands until about twenty to thirty years ago, but then things began to change in several ways. Deep wells became more affordable and cheaper. The management of the tanks was with the local bodies, where rich farmers had a big say. These farmers already had wells and therefore had no interest in maintaining the tanks. Urban construction interfered with water flow into the tanks or the cities diverted the water for consumption.

In those vulnerable environments where wells and canals already became established systems, funding support for watershed management was not available. But states there encouraged new technologies to save on water use.

* * *

The only proven general solutions to water conservation in irrigated agriculture are drips, and sprinkler systems. There is no one type of drip or sprinkler system. Most in use in India are surface drips and not underground drips. All available types share a single objective, to minimize evaporation while delivering the quantity of water that plant roots need. These systems began to be used in India in the early twenty-first century, and since then became popular. As they did, a few Indian companies emerged as the world's leading manufacturers of drip systems.

Most studies of water productivity show that drips and sprinklers are far more productive than traditional flooding type irrigation. Not only do they save on water, but, in some cases, they improve the yield per hectare. They also show productivity to vary between crops, higher in water-intensive crops like sugarcane, banana, and vegetables and lower in the main food crops.[42] These systems involve a large capital expenditure, to begin with. Where states subsidized their installation, drips advanced. Not surprisingly, their use is still limited, to perhaps less than 20 percent of the croplands where drips and sprinklers can be installed. The use is variable too. In the drier states, Maharashtra, Andhra Pradesh, Tamil Nadu, Rajasthan, and Karnataka, drips and sprinklers are used. In Uttar

Pradesh, Punjab, and Haryana, their use is limited. While their use increased, it did not rise enough to make a significant difference to groundwater levels.[43] Why have drips and sprinklers made limited inroads into the most intensively cultivated areas? The big reason is that groundwater is artificially cheap.[44] Wheat and rice still depend on wells and canals. The states sometimes subsidize the water withdrawal from these sources by offering cheap electricity. And as they do, drips have a limited, almost invisible effect on groundwater level and quality.

If all else fails, can law still work? Since around 1970, "model" laws have existed to govern the sinking of wells. As the crisis deepened in the 1990s, the model was revised, with little effect on practice. Making such models into law was not going to be easy and failed in Tamil Nadu state. A potentially more significant step was the model water law drafted in 2017, which declared groundwater a common property, making any user legally bound to agree to shared usage rules. These guidelines ask the state authority to collect regular data and register wells. Whether the 2017 model law made a difference to governance is still too early to say.[45] Case judgments, such as the 2004 one cited at the head of chapter 4, set out an ideal awaiting appropriate enforcement systems.

* * *

This chapter discussed two main fields of conflict over water: sharing of surface water (between nations, provinces, and the city and the farmland) and overuse of groundwater. Politics and institutional change tried to come to grips with these conflicts, with limited success. On a local scale, water markets and cooperation required conditions for their success; some of these conditions were hard to meet. Legal regulation of groundwater moved on without an enforcement infrastructure. What one study calls "the problem of scale" made negotiations a tense process.[46] The problem of scale is a simple one. There is not enough water for everyone. The condition stems from India's geography, but it was made worse by intensive agriculture and by private investment in the cities. And yet, private investment may hold the best promise for the future. State subsidies sometimes encourage waste of water and sometimes encourage economizing. Incentivizing investment in micro-irrigation and taxing the consumption of water-intensive crops could be a way forward.

I have finished the water narrative. How seasonality was overcome is a story that remains to be told.

7

SEASONALITY

In the rainy season there is a wide expanse of water and nothing else.
—Punjab Banking Enquiry, 1929, on land around Delhi city

Seasonal migration of labour . . . is the only alternative to semi-starvation.
—Royal Commission on Agriculture in India, 1928

In 1896, a Bengali gentleman wrote a poem about a group of migrant workers in lower Bengal. "Labourers from the west country" gathering clay from a riverbed was a scene ordinary enough to escape the notice of most Bengalis but fascinated the poet. He observed the children, especially a little girl washing dishes in the river while looking after her even smaller brother. As her parents work, "the girl goes back, the child's hand in her right hand . . . a surrogate of her mother."[1] In fertile and water-rich Bengal, the poorer people lived on land, and most did not leave home. They were poor because the average size of landholding was too small. Still, there was some work to be had throughout the year. Very few provinces in India had that privilege. The poor had little work nearer home and traveled long distances to work in construction sites. In clayey Bengal, bricklayers "from the west" were a familiar sight in the winter months. They moved in families, the adults working and the children minding other children. And they disappeared just before the monsoon rains began.

These seasonal occupations were nothing new in India. But the scale, pattern, and effect had changed since the nineteenth century. The massive expansion of agricultural trade increased the impact of seasons on many livelihoods directly or indirectly dependent on trade. In other words, besides water access, the climate effect began to change in another way. Capital and labor moved around more to reduce the long periods of idleness. The extreme seasonality of tropical monsoon agriculture had imposed such idleness and made people ready to leave the village if there was work outside it. There was work outside the village. Whereas some of these opportunities dried up in the nineteenth century, new fields opened in factories, plantation estates, and commercial agriculture. The railways reduced the cost of making a move, working in a town for part of the year, and returning to the village for a part of the year when agricultural work peaked.

These modern movements had little relation with wages. Wage rates were low and held almost steady. Factory workers could sometimes join unions and wrest some increase. Some skilled artisanal services saw a rise in earnings. Most manual and semiskilled work did not see a noticeable rise in real wages. And yet, people did circulate more than before. They did, economists and Marxist historians think, because there was "surplus" labor in the countryside or the migrants had been forced to move by famines, poverty, or disease. "Unfortunate human beings" was how one study of the jute mill workers of Calcutta described these migrants.[2]

These readings are not persuasive. Migrant labor was never totally surplus back in the village; their work was needed during planting and harvest. Some of the most distressed people in rural India who died during the famines did not come to work in the city factory. Many among those inside the factories in Bombay and Calcutta were landholding peasants, not landless workers. And they were predominantly men, not women. The readiness to migrate had little to do with being "unfortunate." Many mill workers were among the fortunate few who could do two jobs. It was a sign of seasonality. Migrants did not bargain for higher wages but still wanted to move to earn a higher income by using their time better.

Capital, too, felt seasonality. The big field of credit operations since the nineteenth century was funding agricultural trade. Bankers migrated from their original homes and resettled or set up branches in large villages, small towns, and railway station towns. Lending money to farmers who had little collateral was a high-risk business. Loan contracts were legally protected, but the courts were expensive. Most bankers used knowledge of clients and personal connections to do business, with only a few top-end banks using negotiated instruments and bills on an extensive scale. When the harvest was collected, the demand for credit rose so fast that the interest rate increased. The attraction of earning a high rate, and their deep knowledge of one market, discouraged bankers from lending money to industries. In other words, with both capital and labor, the options available to overcome seasonality did not make everyone better-off.

Circulation of labor in southern Asia had a prehistory because the impulse to move was so rooted in climate.

* * *

"Half of India's population" in the eighteenth century, says the historian David Ludden, was mobile, and many were seasonal migrants.[3] Any number on the scale of migration in the eighteenth century is as good as any other. But Ludden sounds right. Throughout India, two occupations—soldiery and construction work—relied on seasonal migrants who came from the farming village in winter and returned there in summer. One of these fields, construction, continued to draw seasonal workers after the advent of British rule. Soldiery ceased to do so.

With its history of famines, South Asia's population always had a significant number of people who were ready to leave the village for months in a year if food and water ran scarce at home and if work was available outside. Such an enormous pool made the states reliant on mercenary soldiers, a much cheaper option than a standing army. The countryside had many people who were not soldiers but who carried arms. In the eighteenth century, as territorial conflicts started breaking out, the soldiers for several rival armies came from such a recruiting pool of part-time peasants.

The military labor market was active throughout the 1700s. Agents and contractors moved around the countryside, recruiting soldiers or negotiating with warlords. With few exceptions, all the significant battles among the British East India Company, the Marathas, Mysore, and Afghan forces in these years took place between October and February. In these months, harvests reached the markets, there was enough food to feed the armies, there was not much farming work to do, and gunpowder stayed dry. Large trains of bullock caravans carrying grain from northern India to the battlefields could move about in winter. Few peasants with arms joined state armies. Most joined small bands under local chiefs and landlords. Some joined ascetic orders like the Dasnamis, also battle-ready for part of the year. These groups, in turn, offered their services to the state armies.

That market started to decline after the company's consolidation as a military power with its takeover of the eastern Indian state of Bengal, around 1765. In most of its early battles, the company relied on part-time peasants from the same stock its allies and rivals depended on, while it also fought with a small regular army. In the longer run, it seemed to act on the belief that a standing army of paid soldiers was a more reliable option and a decisive advantage over the indigenous states, dependent on the uncertain supplies of unreliable mercenaries. From the end of the century, the company fought with a large army, larger than most armies of the indigenous states, all paid from a central treasury and fighting under a central command. Its rivals had little chance of resisting the military machine.

As it consolidated power, the company needed to disarm a vast number of people available for hire. It did partly by monopolizing the market. Instead of offering them jobs only when a war was on or they were unemployed, the company offered its soldiers a year-round salary and a retirement pension in the form of a plot of agricultural land back in the village. The market collapsed, bringing down with it a vast number of intermediaries. "With only one employer left, the role for brokerage, for labour agents and jobber-commanders (*jamadars*) dwindled to almost nil."[4]

The move did not exactly disarm the countryside, however. The new state could not hire all. Those it could not, and demobilized soldiers of the princely states, hung around. The line between banditry and battle had always been a thin one when so many people in the countryside went armed and were unemployed for a long part of the year. Through the early to mid-1800s, the local officers in central, southern, and eastern India were busy suppressing bandits of various sorts, from "thuggees" who preyed on pilgrims and travelers on forested roads, to river pirates in the Bengal delta, to "pindaries," remnants of Afghan cavalry regiments. Whereas such organized predatory groups did retreat into the shadows, they did not disappear.

Nor did the arms. Artisanal production of guns and their use remained widespread. The guns acquired other services, including riots, land disputes, and protection against wild animals. Although the Indian Arms Act of 1878 insisted on a license, it had little effect in the remote countryside. In 1907, Jim Corbett (1875–1955), the hunter and conservationist, was pursuing the Champawat man-eating tiger that had taken hundreds of lives in a remote corner of the Himalayas. At one point, Corbett decided to organize a beat (a mass charge down a forested hill slope to drive animals into the open). This was a dangerous operation for everyone, and few volunteered for it. The local tax officer "had let it be known that he would turn a blind eye towards all unlicensed fire-arms, and further that he would provide ammunition." The incentive worked, "and the weapons that were produced that day would have stocked a museum."[5]

For decades before this incident, soldiery had ceased to be a viable part-time occupation for the seasonally unemployed farmer. But other labor markets were warming up. Massive canal works in the Ganges-Jumna tract in the north, dam building in some of the southern deltas, railways, and expanding cities employed vast numbers of people in brickmaking. Bricks were made in the open air under dry conditions. The work built up from the middle of the monsoon season when recruiting agents became active. At the peak of the season in winter, thousands of people worked on a single site (for example, Roorkee, a Ganges Canal base), producing millions of bricks. Seasonal laborers received higher wages than year-round ones because the former worked hard in backbreaking conditions to take enough money home at the end of the construction season. With the work moving at such a high speed, industrial relations were on edge, as a strike in 1848–1849 showed.[6]

What happened next? Sources on work and the workers suggest that the seasonal element increased in significance in the late nineteenth century and across the board. It did because colonial India experienced an enormous increase in agricultural trade, export of agricultural goods, and the extent of cultivation—a product of a series of changes in technology, institutions, and world markets. A vast range of livelihoods from production to trade to finance became more exposed than before to the seasonal rhythm of agricultural work. So, seasonal circulation of people continued, now on the back of this emerging agricultural economy. A great deal of official documentation about work noticed the pattern and wrote about it. In the following few sections of the chapter, I set out the pattern.

What did extreme seasonality mean in relation to the availability of work? To answer the question, I construct a snapshot from a source published in the 1920s.[7]

* * *

With the arrival of the rains in June from the southwest monsoon, the land in most parts of India was plowed and sown with the monsoon (kharif) crops, which were rice, millets, maize, groundnut (in South India), and cotton. These were rain-fed crops and harvested between August and December. Between October and December, the winter crops, or rabi—wheat, barley, and pulses—were sown. These were harvested in March–April. The peak harvest season occurred in December and March when the largest number of crops came into the markets. The winter crops either were irrigated or made use of the northeast monsoon or reverse monsoon, which brought some moisture in southern coastal India. The northeast monsoon was a weak one but did enable some locally consumed grains.

Not all crops followed these seasonal cycles. Sugarcane was a year-round crop planted in January and harvested the next December. Jute was sown in February and harvested in July. Sugarcane needed heavy irrigation, and jute needed the standing water on lowlands. These, therefore, were planted in small areas. Sugarcane made the winter market busier. The effect of the jute harvest was confined locally.

No region in India produced the full basket of kharif and rabi crops. All regions grew monsoon crops, and areas that received secure irrigation grew winter crops. These areas included Punjab, southwestern coastal deltaic regions, and parts of the Indo-Gangetic basin with many wells. Most areas left a part of the cultivable land fallow during summer. Even in the busiest areas, from March to July was a time of little activity.

In 1954, the government of independent India published the results of the Agricultural Labour Enquiry, the first large-scale survey of the poorest earners of the country. Seasonality was acute, the survey found. The days of complete idleness in a year exceeded one hundred in all but two provinces. Further, the days worked in nonagricultural activity were correlated positively with days worked in agricultural activity. There was also a positive relationship between work intensity and average wages. In other words, nonfarm work was not an independent and paying alternative to farm work. Those who were trapped in a highly rain-dependent agricultural world could not find an escape in nonfarm work. Their only option was to leave and go far away. There was no work near home.

During the monsoon season, peasants needed money to hire extra workers for sowing. Still, the June–July season was weak compared with the peak trading season in winter, when the demand for money to finance commodity trade exploded. Trade became active in winter, not just because there were more articles to trade, but because roads were safer and rivers more navigable in winter. In areas not served by coastal shipping or a railway line, transportation broke down during the monsoon and revived in winter. In deltaic Bengal, the rivers were dangerous to navigate during monsoons. In the plains near Delhi, "in the rainy season there [was] a wide expanse of water and nothing else."[8]

Fishing was a seasonal industry because the overflowing water of the monsoons made fishing dangerous. In the semiarid areas where fodder was scarce, the livestock market moved seasonally. Cattle were sold off to breeders and herders at the end of the sowing season. These herders took cattle nearer forest areas for grazing. They were repurchased before the next sowing season. Trans-frontier trade with Tibet, Afghanistan, and central Asia peaked in winter. Frontier communities such as the Bhotiyas and the Tibetan traders, who were suppliers of wool to the plains, remained in the mountains with their herds, spun wool, and cultivated land during summer. They descended to the plains to trade in large fairs in December and January. Woolen textile mills of North India purchased raw wool from them to make army blankets. Coastal trade became active in winter because coastal shipping routes were safer to operate then.

Consumption varied by season. After the harvest, many marriages took place, stimulating demand for high-quality clothes. The cotton weavers faced idleness in the monsoon months because the market was down and because open-air processing of yarn was not easy in the rains. For the rural poor, the basket of food articles was bigger and more varied in winter.

Because there was a chance to earn extra money, some people moved around. In the western Gangetic plains, migrant agricultural laborers were hired for the rabi sowing, carpenters and blacksmiths hired workers to produce tools, and consumer durables sold in fairs. Forest contractors hired sawyers in October to cut trees in the Himalayan foothills and supply timber to the railways. The timber contractors, therefore, needed to borrow to employ large numbers in winter.

The cotton textile mills of Bombay and Ahmadabad and the jute mills of Calcutta had storages of raw material to keep the workforce engaged throughout the year. But their workers did not want to work throughout the year. The mill worker in Bombay and Calcutta went home to northern India during the sowing season in June and the harvest in winter. Mill managers blamed them for "absenteeism." In the 1950s, American sociologists fascinated by Indian culture took these reports literally and thought that the Indian workers needed to learn modern industrial discipline from Westerners. Many of these workers owned land and had taken loans from traders to finance cultivation back home. They were committed to these traders as well. Likewise, in the off-season, there were reverse movements of people out of the interior into the towns. "The agriculturist," said the inspector of factories in Delhi in 1930, "generally finds attraction for industrial employment *for short periods.*"[9]

Most other factories functioned only in the harvest seasons. About a fifth of the employment in registered factories in 1919, or two to three hundred thousand people, worked for wages in small- and medium-scale units. Such industries clustered in small towns in the interior, for example, gins in Khandesh, grain milling in coastal Andhra, handlooms in western India, bricks and tiles in Malabar, or tanneries in North Arcot, and hired migrants who came from neighboring areas. Grain mills, oil presses, tile and brickmaking, and raw sugar production worked full-time in winter. Cotton gins and jute presses were seasonal activities.

With such modulations in the general economic activity, no wonder anyone whose main work depended in some manner on agriculture would want to create a portfolio of jobs. Such moves almost always entailed migration.

* * *

Persons who declared themselves as "immigrants" formed no more than 1.8–3.0 percent of the total population in 1901–1931. The percentage looks small, but it was made up of five to ten million persons who had moved long distances. Most moved into specific occupations of recent origin. Agriculture rarely offered full-time work for more than 220–240 days in a year, in the dry regions much less. Even though average earnings in the factories of the nineteenth century were marginally higher than what a peasant expected to earn in agriculture, there was work available in mills, mines, and plantations. Even the well-off peasant families could afford to send their adult males off to nonagricultural wage work, recalling them to meet the peak season tasks.

More people moved out of densely populated regions of the Indo-Gangetic basin, where too little land was available per person, or out of arid zones where too little water was available per person. Traders and professionals concentrated in market towns and port cities. In Assam, migrant peasants sought cultivable land. Skilled artisans moved closer to the markets for their goods. Handloom weavers left the dry Deccan trap areas to go to more water-secure towns farther west and resettled as factory owners and factory workers there.[10] There were also movements of agricultural laborers toward new cultivation zones, such as the canal colonies, and into the railways and construction work. The emerging agricultural regions, such as Punjab, did not have a large local labor pool.

Why did people need to go far away from home to find work? After all, their wages were low. What stopped the factories from moving closer to the areas where the low-wage people were? Factories and labor-hiring large businesses had many reasons to locate in a city. They also had a reason to avoid the countryside; there were few consumers there.

What was the problem with consumption?

* * *

The greater the seasonality in agriculture, the smaller the number of working days in the countryside, the more seasonal surplus labor there is. The availability of cheap labor could be an opportunity for an investor in, say, a clothing factory. Historians of early modern Europe and Japan show that the availability of cheap unemployed household labor could be a useful, productive resource for craft-based industrialization. In the 1950s, the economist W. Arthur Lewis constructed a theory of economic development where unemployed rural labor was a useful resource.[11]

In an arid monsoon climate, however, the logic failed. Surplus labor was more a burden than an asset. If agriculture is so monsoon-dependent that there is only one short productive season, then the average yields are too low, marketable surplus too small. Therefore, local demand for textiles is small as well. The local clothing factory would not have much business in such a place. In the arid areas, being agricultural would mean exposure to risk, which reduced expected incomes. A highly seasonal rural economic world was a poor economic world. Since the demand for goods matters, we should not see industry and services flourish just because there was cheap labor among rural families. Industry did grow in the small towns and the port cities. It did not thrive in the countryside. Rural laborers and peasant families did not start weaving high-quality cloth. In the countryside, the number of days of work in industry and services rarely exceeded twenty in a year, the Agricultural Labour Enquiry cited earlier had shown.

Not all the rural world was trapped in such low-productivity and high-risk conditions. After all, commercial agriculture did grow. Between 1870 and 1920, agricultural production and trade increased. Rural incomes grew, if more in some areas. The peasants and workers there did buy more articles. Average cloth consumption increased from six square yards in 1840 to fifteen in 1940. Such an increase in consumption could not just happen by relying on the urban demand for textiles. Peasants, too, bought more cloth and good-quality cloth. In some parts of rural India, they did because incomes grew with irrigation expansion and commercialization of agriculture. But the effect was not strong everywhere.

Even when rural consumption grew, rural production did not. The countryside was not the best place to develop the nonfarm industry. Peasants and laborers had no way of learning a complex craft skill. In the caste-divided society, no artisan would teach them. Instead, they could only move into other forms of labor. Extreme seasonality in the presence of caste biases was not compatible with rural industrialization.

Seasonal unemployment imposed a pattern on those who did move. No one sold land or gave up the chance to earn money from peak season agricultural wages. Where the whole work was seasonal—say, construction or brickmaking—often families migrated for part of the year. Where the work was year-round, men went, and women stayed back. Migration was male-biased because women married early and had children to look after at the same time as they became able to work.[12] The men went to the port city seeking work. The women who stayed behind joined farming work and sought a more casual type of contract. The censuses of colonial India showed a continuous rise in the proportion of agricultural laborers and the feminization of the pool. Early analysts of the employment statistics either read it as a sign of distress or dismissed the feature as a quirk of the statistical system. It was neither. The trend showed how families dealt with seasonality by sending a part of their work capacity away, while retaining control over the rest.

The indirect impact of these movements on the village were deep. Take employment contracts, for example.

* * *

As circulation increased, it changed employment terms in the village. Varieties of obligatory labor started to disappear, although some new forms of debt bondage appeared too. What was obligatory labor? People who were idle for one hundred days in a year were still needed for the few days when sowing or harvesting was done. In India, labor was scarce during the busy seasons. There was little formal slavery in India, but farm servant arrangements and debt bondage were common in the dryland areas of South India.[13] The arrangements worked as insurance for the employers desperate to secure the required number of hands in a few weeks in the farming calendar.

Farm servants in colonial India were not alike. In Madras, they belonged in castes that could not own land. In Punjab, farm servants were cultivators on the side and worked under negotiated contracts. In some parts of central India, farm servants were like apprentices and a prospective groom for the daughter of the family.[14] Madras, not surprisingly, was the driest of these three examples. Despite these differences, there was a single motivation behind the arrangements. On the employers' side, the reason was to avoid a shortage of workers in the peak season. On the workers' side, the arrangement carried the promise of food and water in seasons when there was no work and little water and food.[15] Whether these arrangements stayed intact during famines or collapsed, it is hard to say.

Such labor was obligatory in that it was caste-based and often bordered on serfdom, if not slavery. The workers were attached to plots of land they could not leave. Caste, as we have seen, could make for a weak entitlement to water. A year-round arrangement with someone who had more secure access, therefore, was helpful. Servitudes of these sorts involved a lack of specialization. The workers were attached to the land, but they were available to work in a range of services in the slack season. Economists later called these "beck and call" relationships. These activities were not chosen by the servants but dictated by their employers. These were manual labor and unskilled work, rarely involving more than the most basic tools and skills. Where artisanal activity was a part of the portfolio, such as weaving or leatherwork, the quality of the work was cruder than the work produced by specialist artisans.

Seasonality thus did not mean complete idleness in the slack months; it meant instead performing a different range of tasks or being available for any odd job. The farm servant worked as nonspecialized "general labor."[16] The 1881 census defined general labor as persons who "take to miscellaneous tasks involving as little as possible of anything beyond bodily strength."[17] General labor consisted of persons who did not specialize and moved between agricultural and nonagricultural labor while always sticking to manual labor. Because women were nonspecialized workers, they were often counted as general labor in the nineteenth-century censuses.

With more circulation opportunities, the average duration of employment contracts began to decline in rural India in the late nineteenth century. The percentage of farm servants in agricultural labor families fell everywhere. In Madras, where farm servant contracts were prevalent, the fall was dramatic. General labor was shrinking in scale in the late colonial times, so that in 1901 the census gave up using the classification category.[18] After the 1950s, official sources discarded the term *attached* laborer: "[For] attached labour is no longer attached to any particular household in the old sense. Such attachments are now conditioned more by economic considerations and may not extend beyond a season or a year at the most."[19]

These arrangements crumbled away because a remarkable fall in migration costs enabled the search for other alternatives. There was more to the change. By the end of the nineteenth century, more of the poorest people than before would have access to the water-secure environments of the city. Therefore, one condition for entering year-round commitments—securing access to food and water if food and water ran out in the dry season—did not operate as powerfully as it did before.

Did the picture change after 1947?

* * *

Good histories of labor market institutions after 1947 remain scarce. We do know that around independence in 1947, the factory workforce had grown roots in the city. All along, hundreds of factories processing agricultural raw material or other natural resources worked during certain seasons. There was a massive increase in construction activity and, with it, brickmaking. Many seasonal migrants joined construction work. There is still a scarcity of research on such forms of activity in India. Isolated academic studies confirm that seasonality matters to employment.[20] Many of India's vast army of self-employed and casual informal workers "both hire in and hire out labour according to seasonal peaks."[21] There are studies on circular migration suggesting that circulation is a typical work-life pattern. Indeed, it may be growing in extent. Seasonality, these works show, pushed people to seek work for part of the year.[22] An ethnographic study on Gujarat over 1981–1997 showed that seasonal migration was pervasive at the end of the 1990s, and migrants went long distances for work. During these years, the areas where they traveled from had industrialized. The employers, instead of hiring locally, preferred to hire migrants over whom they had more power.[23]

In the semiarid regions, seasonality created various stresses, idleness, poverty of natural resources, and the risk of falling into debt to meet temporary hardships.[24] Poor people are not poor forever. Those who gain in one good year can fall into poverty again in a bad year in the water-short regions. They worked in seasonal factories and construction sites. Such workplaces, being temporary, did not or cannot work by legal rules. A permanent worksite would not hire seasonal migrants. In other words, even as more people worked, more people worked under quite difficult, and dangerous, conditions. Construction workers until recently came to the cities with families and had their children living and playing near the sites. In both colonial and postcolonial India, being able to migrate was a step to avoid being deprived of food and water and sometimes earn extra money to educate children. It was, however, not a safe way to overcome poverty.

Workers still could take chances. Capitalists had more to lose by taking chances. And yet they, too, faced seasonality.

* * *

Between 1870 and 1930, agricultural production in India grew by 50–100 percent, thanks to the railways and the new irrigation projects (chapter 4). The growth in agricultural trade needed bigger flows of credit. Between 1870 and 1930, the volume of credit linked to agricultural trades increased by 200–300 percent in real terms. The indigenous bankers, operating as family firms, met the need for credit well enough. Most of these firms dealt with the local merchants, and some with the peasants. On the other side, corporate banks and bigger indigenous firms based in the cities dealt with the small-scale bankers' needs for money.

People in the countryside needed to borrow for three reasons: to finance production, trade, or consumption. Each one of these activities was distinct from the others. Financing production and trade were both seasonal, but the seasons did not overlap. Peasants borrowed during the planting season in July to hire laborers and bullock, and buy seeds, material, and food. They paid off the loan in December or January. Usually, their lenders were not professional bankers. The neighborhood landlord, rich farmer, or grain merchants gave these loans. Such people had a stake in the grain trade. When the loan was repaid, grain prices were lower than they were in July. The lender could profit from that price difference. It was difficult, therefore, to calculate the interest rate on production loans exactly. The second type, trade credit, was offered to merchants in December and January, and repaid a few months later. Professional bankers had a large role in this market. The third type, consumption loan, depended less on the season and more on the circumstances of the borrower. Still, during years when the harvest failed, many people needed to borrow for this reason and sell land or jewelry to repay the loan. Most descriptions of the financial market in this chapter relate to the second type of credit.

As the banking business became more tied to commodity trade, the seasonal influence on the financial market increased. One of the first systematic histories of Indian banking, from 1864, did not mention the words *season* and *rain*. In contrast, the evidence collected by the Banking Enquiry Commission in 1929–1930 used these words hundreds of times.[25] A large amount of the cash reserves of banks converted into trade credit during the winter months. The apex bank, the

Imperial Bank (formed of the Presidency Banks, discussed below) increased its rate to protect its reserves. During the primary harvest season (January–March), demand for money was at its peak, and loan rates between traders and peasants could be as high as 12–24 percent, even among known clients. By April, the market started cooling. In the rains (June–August) the rates crashed, and money markets disintegrated as movements of capital between small and large centers reduced.

The Imperial Bank's rate was a kind of bank rate influencing other rates. It saw big fluctuations between seasons. The rate ranged between 4 and 10 percent in the 1870s. As corporate banking and the bill market expanded, there was some moderation in the seasonal effect. The peaks and troughs came closer, and the average monthly interest rate fell during 1870–1920. There was more money coming into the system, and it was circulating between seasons better than before. Not enough, though, to remove the pattern.

A market in bills or promises to pay should make more people lend money rather than hoard money. Thanks to the law of negotiable instruments, bills did circulate more than before, and the links between corporate banks and local bankers did get closer over time. The effect was modest nonetheless. Lenders in agricultural credit did not transact using bills. Their clients did not understand or accept papers, and the courts of law and discounting counters were too distant. The local financial markets dealt with only physical money.

Beyond the general features of the financial market, the market was quite complex internally. For example, it had several actors who did not face seasonality quite in the same way or respond to it in the same way. Who were they?

* * *

Corporate banking began in the early nineteenth century. Corporate banks included the foreign-owned exchange banks, licensed to deal in foreign currency transactions; the partly government-owned Presidency Banks; and other banks. There was also a mixed set of cooperative credit societies, loan offices, and land mortgage banks. The Presidency Banks were the Bank of Bengal, established in 1806; the Bank of Bombay, 1840; and the Bank of Madras, 1843. These functioned as the government's banker and were amalgamated to form the Imperial Bank in 1921. These banks handled domestic trade and remittance and accepted bills issued by the indigenous bankers. Most were based in the port cities.

Indian merchants and landlords frequently floated banks. Only a few of these survived the worst business cycles. Most small banks depending on local savings suffered from a high death rate. There was a high incidence of insider lending in these businesses; that is, bankers lent to firms that they owned, or their friends did. Corporate banks dealt in other people's money. A weak regulatory system encouraged fraud and waste. When a merchant combine floated a bank, invariably lot of the money went to the same trades that these owners were interested in.

There was another reason for the high mortality. No surprise here. It was extreme seasonality. There was a disparity between the assets and the liabilities of these banks. Most of their loans went to businesses affected by seasonality. In a bad harvest year, a lot of the loans went bad. The obligation to pay interest on deposits remained intact. The outflow was not a seasonal one; the inflow was seasonal. If a bank suffered a loss in one year due to a harvest failure and unpaid debts, the rumor it might sink would cause a run on the deposits and ensure it did sink.

Noncorporate family firms were not so vulnerable because they did business based on their own savings and profits. Indeed, most such bankers avoided getting involved in the deposit business and thus taking on a nonseasonal liability. Indigenous banking firms belonged to the families that had been doing the business for generations. Many were earlier based in towns situated on the overland and river-borne trade routes, such as Benares, Mathura, Delhi, or Jaipur. In the eighteenth and nineteenth centuries, many of these families relocated to the port cities, Bombay, Calcutta, and Madras. The bankers belonged in certain castes and communities, the prominent among these being the Multani and the Marwari, the Bengali Saha, the Nattukottai Chettiar, Kallidaikurichi Brahmins in South India, the Jains and Gujaratis in Bombay, and Rohilla Afghans. The small group of income tax payers in the 1920s consisted of a few of these bankers.

The biggest of these firms funded export trade, funded other bankers, sometimes did some deposit business, and were somewhat less susceptible to seasonality. They also dealt in bills, called hundis. The ordinary meaning of *hundi* was "banker's draft" or "promissory note," though sometimes merchants' bills of exchange were also called hundis. An important piece of British Indian legislation, the Negotiable Instruments Act of 1881, covered some types of hundis.[26] The reputation of the acceptors as banking houses and the customary law and conventions they followed ensured that the corporate banks discounted the hundis they issued.

The dealings between the lender and the borrower closer to agricultural land were less diversified and fiercely seasonal.

These parties dealt in cash because their clients could not write a contract, or a bill market was not accessible. Most loans were unsecured because the peasants could not furnish worthwhile security. Unsecured loans paid out in cash to poor borrowers exposed to floods or droughts carried high risks. Therefore, the peak season interest rate rose to very high levels, usually 12–24 percent per annum, in arid areas reaching three or four times that. The rates dropped to 4–6 percent in the off-season. Demand for money fell. The lenders hoarded cash in readiness for the next busy season.

There were two types of risk in the business, not knowing the debtor well enough, or asymmetric information as economists call it, and not being able to predict the quality of the harvest season. Economists do not have a name for the second risk because they have not studied climatic risk in credit markets enough. Climatic risk is not a serious problem for the Western world, which is the world most economists are accustomed to studying.

Asymmetric information was easier to address. Every member of every set selected their clients based on personal information. For example, the indigenous bankers charged lower rates for transactions among members of their own caste or community. A Marwari banker explained, "They know the people they are dealing with."[27] In western India, "a remarkable feature of the indigenous banking system [was that the banker knew] the history of the family of his borrower."[28] In big deals, a certain degree of transparency was maintained. "Indigenous bankers deal principally with men of business or the educated."[29] The Chettiar bankers lent money only "relying on their estimate of their clients' worth and reputation among their banking community."[30] The European bankers of Calcutta were friendly with the European clients, not only because they played golf together on Sundays, but also because the bankers knew how to read their client companies' accounts. Many Indian firms would not show their books to the corporate bankers, or the latter would not understand the accounts. The interest rate depended on such knowledge, or "interest on unsecured loan depend[ed] on the character of the borrower."[31]

However, a lot of the risk did not stem from lack of information but was seasonal. No amount of information on the client's accounts or trustworthiness could mitigate the risk of a bad season, which would bring the debtor down and the lender with him or her. Nobody could predict the season. Most local loans were unsecured and not mortgage-backed. As one bank officer of Bengal reported, "It may be safely assumed that 50 per cent of such loans . . . becomes ultimately irrecoverable."[32] Even if the percentage is an exaggeration, the risk was no doubt high.

The big city bankers had a diversified portfolio to mitigate such risks. Their clients included landlords; warehouse owners; merchants with personal reputation; agents of outstation trading firms; tea estates; traders buying jute, tobacco, and chilli crops where these profitable cash crops were grown; and urban services such as cinema and theater industries. They discounted bills of exchange and issued remittance instruments such as commercial papers when they were branches of Bombay or Calcutta firms. The Chettiar bankers transferred funds in the slack season to Rangoon, Malaya, and the Straits Settlements.[33]

The local bankers, by contrast, had little defense against seasonal risk. Bills failed to circulate below the banker-to-banker level, leading contemporary critics of Indian banking to complain of "inelasticity" of the supply of money in response to trade demand.[34] The hundi was rarely used between the grain merchant and the bankers. As in every other partially legislated customary instrument, its acceptance depended on personal knowledge and personal security. The reach of that knowledge was limited. Law was ambiguous. "There is no legal definition of a *hundi*."[35] As court cases showed, contract enforcement often depended on the meaning of the hundi in particular contexts.[36] They were cashable only in the town mentioned in the document. Few bankers entertained a hundi without personal knowledge of the drawee. The diverse profile of the lenders, many of whom were merchants and bankers of small resources, and immense variation in local conventions made designing a proper legal framework for bills a frustrating enterprise. Therefore, the financial system was not well equipped to spread credit between seasons and types of borrowers.

Local bankers dealt in cash, therefore. "During the busy season when demand for cash is great, bankers keep as high a cash balance as possible."[37] Most loans were unsecured. Even when loans were secured, taking possession of mortgaged assets was not easy. Land mortgage deals were covered in several provinces by laws preventing land transfer. These laws stemmed from a pervasive anxiety among the officers. The colonial contract law, they felt, had empowered the moneylenders and weakened the peasants, who paid the taxes. Driven by the sentiment, legislation turned debtor-friendly, and creditors faced high transaction costs in settling a debt suit. By confining the mortgage market thus, the law ensured the mortgage deeds were not tradable instruments.[38] The banker's defense was to factor in all sorts of risks—weather, poverty of the client, cost of enforcing contracts—into the busy season interest rate, which rose to high levels.

Such a season-bound financial market excluded many types of borrowers whose investments would have sustained businesses outside agriculture. I discuss some instances of the syndrome next.

* * *

"There is at present [in the 1920s] a complete divorce between banks and industry."[39] Despite the growth of their business, neither the corporate banks nor the family firms invested money in the modern industry. Why did they not? To whom could industries turn for long-term credit?

Big companies of Calcutta floated shares and used their own reserves to fund investment. They borrowed from corporate banks to finance working capital. Companies of Bombay and Ahmadabad were more successful in attracting deposits from indigenous bankers. Several so-called swadeshi, or nationalistic, banks floated in Bengal in the wake of the freedom movement moved into industrial financing. Most of them failed. Small and medium firms, therefore, borrowed from friends and relations or from their buyers.

To take on any extraordinary investment commitments, such firms needed to borrow at dangerously high rates. An example will illustrate the problem. In Assam, tea estates were owned by European companies. In the Dooars region of Bengal, estates of small size were owned by Bengali professionals. Both the European estates and the Bengali estates sold tea in the Calcutta auctions, but the latter found it difficult to get financing. The bigger estates could establish a brand for their tea and get funded by banks and the tea auction firms. Makers of unbranded tea had little clout with the auction houses.

When they borrowed money, these estates borrowed from Marwari bankers at rates reaching the peak season agricultural rate.[40]

Why would bankers prefer to keep money idle for several months in a year instead of lending long-term? Their knowledge network included commodity traders and not industrialists. Industrial investment tied up money, and no banker wanted to miss the chance of making a killing in the busy agricultural season. Even though there was plenty of money available for lending, in the slack season "it [was] not possible to utilise these funds . . . as the money [was] required by [the bankers] in the [busy] season."[41]

What happened to financial markets after 1947?

* * *

Concerns with seasonality dropped out of public discourse in the 1950s. Rural credit surveys and Reserve Bank of India (the central bank, started in 1935) documents acknowledged seasonality but noted it as a fact of life. The Reserve Bank commissioned some works measuring seasonality in commodity prices. These studies offered mixed results on whether the extent of seasonality declined or stayed the same.[42] None of these works said why seasonality might be a problem beyond banks' liquidity management or technical exercises such as money demand estimation.

There is a reason for the oversight. Both commodity trade and banking were nationalized in a series of moves after 1950. Most indigenous banking firms disappeared, and members of these communities shifted occupations. Private moneylending came under a slew of restrictive laws. Interest rates came to be controlled, and seasonal variations were officially abolished, or so the economists believed. In the 1980s, microfinance institutions took away some of the businesses the informal lenders did earlier. The informal money market did not disappear, but it lay so low that the government and the central bank could not see them or collect much information on them.

Needless to say, seasonality did not disappear. Cash and gold transactions still rise in India during the harvest season because the busy agricultural season coincides with festivals and weddings. The popular press in India is full of reports on how moneylending not only survives the progress of formal finance but even flourishes by moving its business online. Little of these reports suggests where most of the money goes to, funding consumption or funding investment.

* * *

Agriculture in a tropical monsoon climate exposed labor and capital to exceptional levels of seasonality. Seasonality enforced unemployment, poverty, and underinvestment. These conditions eased a great deal after the late nineteenth century. The cities and commercial agriculture drew a section of the rural population toward new jobs. But the trend increased inequality. Men migrated more. Peasants moved into the factories more than agricultural laborers. As rural consumption increased, the specialist artisan gained because new consumption goods embodied skills. The general laborers or farm servants could find it difficult to acquire these skills. They went into other forms of labor.

The growth of commercial agriculture similarly had an inequality effect on the financial market. Like the workers, bankers moved around, became deeply involved with agriculture, and thus were more exposed to seasonality. One short-term market made such a massive draft on available money as to crowd out the other potential users of money. The credit market for long-term loans was undeveloped. Loans of the duration of more than one year were hard to find. For any term longer than one season, the lender insisted on collateral such as gold jewelry. In many provinces, debt laws immobilized the land mortgage market. Having to deal with seasonality made banks unsuitable agents to fund industrialization. Financial modernization happened, but with one hand tied to agricultural finance, whereas legislation played an incomplete and often reactionary role.

Chapters 2–7 developed a narrative of economic change. Chapter 8 returns to the theme of geographical agency in modern history. It returns to the concept of tropical monsoon economies. I ask: In the presence of the pervasive and profound influence of geography on economic change, how should we write the history of economic change? Chapter 8 answers the question.

8

MONSOON ECONOMIES

This book has lessons for those interested in knowing how geography shaped economic change in the monsoon-tropical lands. The influence was great and systematic, and no account of long-run economic change in southern Asia or the world should overlook the effect.

The book has implications of a methodological kind. It matters to know, I claim, why geography matters at all. And it matters to the way we understand and discuss environmental change and the sustainability of economic growth. The last chapter is about these lessons.

I start with a summary of the arguments.

* * *

The South Asians experienced the tropical monsoon climate as a barrier to sustainable economic and population growth. Life and work before 1850 relied on a climate pattern that entailed pervasive unemployment and drought risk. The monsoon enabled any agriculture at all in these arid areas of the world. And yet, unemployment was built into the agricultural regime because it depended on a short rain-fed cultivation season. Drought risk came from variations in the volume and timing of rainfall against excessive heat. These conditions did not influence equally all parts of the large region. The seaboard was less susceptible to these risks. The Indo-Gangetic basin or the deltas had conditions more suitable for intensive agriculture. These were not the norm, and disasters elsewhere could upset the less vulnerable regions too.

The nineteenth-century forces transforming the world economy—trade, technology, urbanization, colonialism, struggles for liberty and equality—enabled a series of interventions that weakened these limits on life and work. These interventions turned controllable water sources for agriculture and consumption into a public and semipublic good, enabling a rise in the capacity of the economy to grow food, sustain population growth, and generate urban growth. Water extraction and access, in this way, played as important a role in Indian economic history as fossil fuel extraction played in the economic emergence of western Europe. Large water projects, the shift of famine-policy focus from food to water, law, movements for equality of access to water, fall in the cost of migration, and growth of financial institutions made the economic revolution possible. People lived longer and moved around more in search of work.

That enormous achievement came with a price. The interventions enabling water-dependent economic change gave rise to stress. Making water rights more inclusive than before saved lives but made the exhaustion of a precious resource more likely. Migration made it possible for unemployed people to move out of seasonal jobs to year-round ones. Not everyone could do so. Gender and skills restricted choices for many. South Asia in the twenty-first century has seen both more water stress and more inequality because of the persistent effects of these factors.

Would climate change make the growth process less sustainable?

* * *

The past meets the future in an environmentally aware history of economic change, as this one aims to be. For measuring global changes in environmental quality, the concept of land now includes water. In the measurements used to map land quality changes, biomass, biodiversity, soil quality, and water together indicate the capacity of land to sustain growing populations without one or more of these attributes degrading. The capacity is low, to begin with, in the arid and semiarid regions of the world, making both population growth and expansion of natural resource–based livelihoods invariably destabilizing. Climate change adds a further element of uncertainty to the equation.

Controlling for climate, the Land Degradation Assessment in Drylands, a policy and data tool devised by the Food and Agriculture Organization (FAO) and its collaborators, shows that much of South Asia can be classified as low capacity with medium to strong levels of degradation at work.[1] The eastern Indo-Gangetic basin is a high-capacity region with medium to strong levels of degradation, whereas much of the Deccan plateau, the Gujarat peninsula, and Pakistan fall in the world's most vulnerable zones. These global data are not of direct interest to the book. But the point that the low capacity of the land to sustain an ecosystem is a structural and inherited condition in South Asia is vital for the book to suggest why the economic processes and water-use processes dealt with herein might not be sustainable.

Would these sustainability challenges increase with global warming? Predictions about the hydrological impact of a rise in global temperature on the monsoon tropics are anything but definitive. A pattern does emerge, however, from the many studies on India done in the past decade. For example, the flow in rivers is expected to increase in May–July and is expected to fall below current levels in the dry months. Himalayan snowmelt water should increase in volume, the monsoon should be rainier and stormier, and summers should be more arid.[2] While these predictions do suggest more uncertainty and sharper seasonal variations, they do not add up to uniformly greater scarcity or greater abundance of water. It is hard to predict what impact the total effect will have on water access on average or water stress.

There would be second-order effects. Warming of the climate and rainfall variability between seasons, causing hotter summers than usual and stronger and extended monsoons, should upset the current crop regimes. For example, rice cultivation using monsoon rainfall could get more difficult, and rice cultivation in summer using groundwater could extend further.[3] Rice, I have shown, has had a disastrous impact on groundwater levels already.

One thing seems inevitable: the dependence on underground water will increase. Groundwater dependence should rise because of increased aridity, which would mean reduced flow in rivers post-monsoon. Some of the existing storage systems such as the human-made lakes, or tanks, of South India would become nonviable or expensive to maintain. The available models do not tell us much about how the recharge capacity of aquifers will change. On that effect, the overall stress will depend a lot.

From the future, I return to the past and ask what lessons historians can learn from tropical monsoon economies.

That many of the world's dryland regions are structurally distinct from western Europe or North America, where the low-capacity high-degradation syndrome rarely appears, makes comparisons between world regions on their ability to generate economic growth quite difficult. Economic historians do not realize how difficult the task is. Moving on to the methodological lessons, I start with economic history.

* * *

Economic history is an inquiry into the roots of growth and inequality. An exciting enterprise, its methods are not without fault. Economic historians often ask why some countries grew rich and others stayed poor from the beginning of the nineteenth century, when trade, cross-border investment, and industrialization raised average productivity manifold. The index to measure economic growth, forging ahead and falling behind, is the average or per capita income.

The usual way to answer the question is to first explain the western European nations' success in raising average income. Armed with a Europeanist account of success, the historians explain the rest of the world's failure to raise incomes by showing what the Europeans did, which the other societies failed to do. The answer varies from the discovery of the institutions of capitalism to the ability to exercise military and naval power over the rest of the world, and many variations of these two themes. In every case, the rest of the world emerges as the less agile of the two parties.

The method is flawed. For it assumes that the geographical conditions are similar enough between these units of comparison. If the world's regions experienced geography differently—some as a facilitator of economic growth and others as an obstacle—one case does not offer a useful lesson for the others.

Regions do differ a lot in their geographies. Much of the world is dry. Western Europe, Japan, and North America are the exceptions. For the rest of the world, the societies' ability to control water determined their ability to generate population and economic growth. Of course, western Europe, North America, and Japan saw more economic growth in modern times. They were lucky. They did not have to worry about securing lives against the threat of a water famine. There is no puzzle there. The rest of the world was not lucky. The immediate challenge there was to prevent deaths from sudden acute shortages of water. The economic emergence of regions facing a binding water constraint is the real puzzle of global economic history.

The argument exposes the book to a potential attack: What about regions within India that did not face the threat of water famine or seasonality to the same extent as the drylands did? Did they grow rich? Indeed, water security was not sufficient for income growth, though it was a necessary condition. Further, areas in India abundant in water were abundant in surface water. In a monsoon environment, dependence on surface water came with the risk of floods. During most of the colonial times, water-rich Bengal did not see a famine. It did see a lot of floods. But floods, while destroying assets, did not kill as many people as a famine. The resultant population growth placed intense pressure on limited land without any addition to the productive power of land. The options to invest in land improvement were expensive. The dam technology did not work well in the soft soil and the flat terrain of the delta. Controllability of water application, I have argued, was necessary for intensive cultivation. In most places, small-scale irrigation systems did not meet the condition (not until the 1980s).

These remarks make the measurement of economic change more complicated than economic historians think it is. Most economists measure desired economic change by average or per capita income. The average is total income divided by population. If a society manages to reduce deaths and improve life spans, the average will be depressed. Economic historians would conclude that such a society was a tragic failure and explain the tragedy by citing some positives happening in Europe and missing in the poorer countries. Missing, because either the societies there were too backward or the European imperialists ruling these places denied them the benefits of Western civilization.

The book rejects these clichés. I call the dynamic, which delivered longer lives, the first condition for economic emergence. India met the condition from around the recent famine era. Water scarcity was mitigated enough to reduce famines and diseases. Despite that enormous positive change, the degree of access to controllable water did not develop fast enough to spread intensive cultivation. The productivity of croplands remained low. The average income curve stayed flat. And yet, by changing the agency of water, Indians solved a problem that was not Europe's problem.

The proposition that water control should be a benchmark of performance frees up global economic history from the sterile Europe-Asia comparison and enables comparisons among the drier regions. For example, the evaporation map of the world tells us that the arid tropics, the so-called monsoon Asia, and the monsoon tropics like South Asia or the Sahel share some similarities and some differences in their ability to control water. Did their economic pathways differ too? Were these more similar than different? Did the differences stem from geography? Did colonialism and globalization affect these regions differently or similarly?

Moving on, the book has a message for discourses on stress and sustainability.

* * *

The power of hydraulics to grow more food enabled a growing population and more jobs. The same process created more pressure on the commons. Economic growth in a water-scarce society is subject to sustainability barriers water-rich societies do not face. What does *sustainability* mean in the context of this study? It is a diverse concept, of course. That is, it means different things in different geographies. Most often, the word conjures up a narrative of unrestrained private greed (capitalism), destroying biodiversity, polluting air, and causing climate change. My account of sustainability has nothing in common with this narrative of an avoidable greed-fueled global disaster in the making.

This particular narrative rules sentiments because much of the ongoing discourses on stress remain trapped in a tragedy-of-the-commons rhetoric. A maxim emerged from Garrett Hardin's framing of the problem: "Freedom in the commons brings ruin to all." The maxim has had enormous influence in shaping activism. It strengthened the belief that market-driven economic change threatened the commons. Capitalism was destroying the earth. The threat is real. And yet, *tragedy* is not the right word to use every time the threat materializes. The word is misplaced with water stress in the tropical monsoon regions, where "freedom in the commons" raised the survival chances of many and brought prosperity to some.[4] Increasing water access involved deliberate democratization of rights to access and a change from the old rules sanctioning segregation, inequity, and inequality. It is "freedom" in a substantive sense but not in Hardin's sense. It is freedom as freer access to a basic human entitlement, not the freedom to destroy.

The equivalence of water access and human freedom suggests that sustainability in the tropical monsoon areas is a more complex affair than many activists realize. They are too obsessed with greenhouse gas and overconsumption to notice the different set of challenges water entails. In a dry region, there is a trade-off between welfare and the environment. Asking water-stressed individuals to consume less is not a persuasive response to the problem. Cooperation and regulation are necessary, of course. So are science and capitalism—the mechanisms that work behind drip irrigation, for one example.

NOTES

SERIES FOREWORD

1. Eric Hobsbawm, *Age of Extremes: The Short Twentieth Century, 1914–1991* (London: Abacus, 1995).

2. Amitav Ghosh, *The Great Derangement: Climate Change and the Unthinkable* (Chicago: University of Chicago Press, 2016).

3. Laura Marris, "Extremotolerance," *Believer*, April 7, 2021, https://believermag.com/logger/extremotolerance/. I am grateful to Akin Akinwumi for bringing this essay to my attention.

4. For an account of emergent resource scarcities and their violent consequences in the climate-changing tropical world, see Christian Parenti, *Tropic of Chaos: Climate Change and the New Geography of Violence* (New York: Nation Books, 2011).

5. Sunil Amrith, *Unruly Waters: How Rains, Rivers, Coasts, and Seas Have Shaped Asia's History* (New York: Basic Books, 2018); Mike Davis, *Late Victorian Holocausts: El Niño Famines and the Making of the Third World* (London: Verso, 2001); Priya Satia, *Time's Monster: How History Makes History* (Cambridge, MA: Belknap Press of Harvard University Press, 2020).

6. There is a branch of investigation and analysis here that tempts further discussion of the more recent recognition by the United Nations General Assembly and the Human Rights Council of water as a human right, which became a part of binding international law.

7. The impact of the Industrial Revolution and the rise of the fossil economy have received extensive attention in recent years, and I could cite numerous works that would far exceed the space afforded to my

preamble in this book. Suffice for me to acknowledge that I draw the term *fossil capital* from Andreas Malm, *Fossil Capital: The Rise of Steam Power and the Roots of Global Warming* (London: Verso, 2016).

8. For an introduction to dam construction in modern India, see Satyajit Singh, *Taming the Waters: The Political Economy of Large Dams in India* (Delhi: Oxford University Press, 1997); and Kathleen D. Morrison, "Dharmic Projects, Imperial Reservoirs, and New Temples of India: An Historical Perspective on Dams in India," *Conservation and Society* 8, no. 3 (2010): 182–195.

9. The notion that the successes and failures of human civilizations can be characterized by, and told through, their challenges to the carrying capacity of regions, nations, continents, or the planet is one of the oldest and most omnipresent tenets of environmental history. Recently, it has been aptly summarized in Donald Worster, *Shrinking the Earth: The Rise and Decline of American Abundance* (New York: Oxford University Press, 2016); and Elizabeth Kolbert, *Under a White Sky: The Nature of the Future* (London: Bodley Head, 2021).

10. Ugo Bardi, *The Seneca Effect: Why Growth Is Slow but Collapse Is Rapid* (New York: Springer, 2017).

11. Marris, "Extremotolerance."

1 WHY CLIMATE MATTERS

1. I borrow the phrase from Swaminathan S. Anklesaria Aiyar, "Drought Not a Big Calamity in India Anymore," *Swaminomics* (blog), *Times of India*, July 29, 2012, https://timesofindia.indiatimes.com/blogs/Swaminomics/drought-not-a-big-calamity-in-india-anymore/.

2. "Why India Needs to Worry about Climate Change," *BBC News*, October 25, 2018, https://www.bbc.co.uk/news/world-asia-india-45949323.

3. Mark Christopher, *Water Wars: The Brahmaputra River and Sino-Indian Relations* (Newport, RI: US Naval War College, 2013), 12.

4. The choice of the starting point is driven by the kind of sources I use herein, which acquire a great deal of depth and density with the reports and evidence of the 1880 Famine Commission.

5. Navin Singh Khadka, "India Water Crisis Flagged Up in Global Report," *BBC News*, August 6, 2019, https://www.bbc.com/news/world-asia-india-49232374.

6. Markus Kottek, Jürgen Grieser, Christoph Beck, Bruno Rudolf, and Franz Rubel, "World Map of the Köppen-Geiger Climate Classification Updated," *Meteorologische Zeitschrift* 15, no. 3 (2006): 259–263, http://koeppen-geiger.vu-wien.ac.at/present.htm.

7. Elements of the tropical monsoon conditions exist in other geographies. We should still be careful not to place all tropical regions and all monsoon regions in one basket. The world's monsoon regions are not alike. If South Asia and northeastern Asia are not comparable, nor are South Asia and the Sahel. The Sahel has a monsoon like India's, but a weaker one. The mean annual rainfall in the Sahel is 100–300 millimeters, in India 300–650 millimeters. Both areas face a high seasonal cost of accessing water, but South Asia has more water.

8. Transpiration from plants also affects the evaporation rate. However, the evaporation data I cite in this discussion do not account for transpiration.

9. M. F. Quamar and S. K. Bera, "Vegetation and Climate Change during Mid and Late Holocene in Northern Chhattisgarh (Central India) Inferred from Pollen Records," *Quaternary International* 349 (2014): 357–366.

10. See discussion in Mayank Kumar, "Invisible–Visible: Sources, Environment and Historians," in *Critical Themes in Environmental History of India*, ed. Ranjan Chakrabarti (New Delhi: Sage, 2020), 17–50.

11. Stephen Broadberry, Johann Custodis, and Bishnupriya Gupta, "India and the Great Divergence: An Anglo-Indian Comparison of GDP Per Capita, 1600–1871," *Explorations in Economic History* 55, no. 1 (January 2015): 58–75. The article contains a useful discussion of other statistical works of a similar nature.

12. W. H. Moreland, *From Akbar to Aurangzeb: A Study in Indian Economic History* (London: Macmillan, 1923), 200. See also W. H. Moreland, "The Ain-i-Akbari—a Base-Line for the Economic History of India," *Indian Journal of Economics* 1 (1917–1918): 44–53. Francisco Pelsaert, *Jahangir's India: The "Remonstrantie" of Francisco Pelsaert*, trans. W. H. Moreland and P. Geyl (Cambridge, UK: W. Heffer and Sons, 1925), 64.

13. India, *Imperial Gazetteer of India*, vol. 3, *Economic* (London: HMSO, 1909), 92.

14. A tank in South India is a human-made reservoir, sometimes embanked.

15. Tim Dyson, *A Population History of India: From the First Modern People to the Present Day* (Oxford: Oxford University Press, 2018).

16. World Bank, "Level of Water Stress: Freshwater Withdrawal as a Proportion of Available Freshwater Resources," https://data.worldbank.org/indicator/ER.H2O.FWST.ZS; World Resources Institute, "Water Stress by Country," https://www.wri.org/resources/charts-graphs/water-stress-country.

17. Eric Jones, *The European Miracle: Environments, Economies, and Geopolitics in the History of Europe and Asia*, 2nd ed. (New York: Cambridge University Press, 1987), 193.

18. Andrew C. Isenberg, ed., *The Oxford Handbook of Environmental History* (Oxford: Oxford University Press, 2017). Several essays in Paul G. Harris and Graeme Lang, eds., *Routledge Handbook of Environment and Society in Asia* (Abingdon: Routledge, 2014), recognize water access, water stress, seasonality, and the institutional challenges involved in dealing with climate change and water stress but do not offer a coherent model of economic history. Constance Lever-Tracy, ed., *Routledge Handbook of Climate Change and Society* (Abingdon: Routledge, 2010), is less useful on monsoon seasonality and is similarly preoccupied with the present. Sam White, Christian Pfister, and Franz Mauelshagen, eds., *The Palgrave Handbook of Climate History* (London: Palgrave, 2018), has excellent essays on South Asia but is sparse on the impact of climate on water and society.

19. Diana K. Davis, *The Arid Lands: History, Power, Knowledge* (Cambridge, MA: MIT Press, 2016).

20. Sunil Amrith, *Unruly Waters: How Mountain Rivers and Monsoons Have Shaped South Asia's History* (London: Penguin, 2018).

21. For surveys, see Mahesh Rangarajan, "Environment and Ecology under British Rule," in *India and the British Empire*, ed. Douglas Peers and Nandini Gooptu (Oxford: Oxford University Press, 2012), 212–230; and Richard Grove, Vinita Damodaran, and Satpal Sangwan, introduction to *Nature and the Orient: The Environmental History of South and Southeast Asia*, ed. Richard Grove, Vinita Damodaran, and Satpal Sangwan (New Delhi: Oxford University Press, 2000), 1–26.

22. David Gilmartin, "Water and Waste: Nature, Productivity and Colonialism in the Indus Basin," *Economic and Political Weekly* 38, no. 48 (November 29, 2003): 5057–5065; Rohan D'Souza, "Water in British

India: The Making of a 'Colonial Hydrology,'" *History Compass* 4, no. 4 (July 2006): 621–628.

23. Harry T. Oshima, *Economic Growth in Monsoon Asia: A Comparative Study* (Tokyo: University of Tokyo Press, 1987).

24. Garrett Hardin, "The Tragedy of the Commons," *Science*, n.s., 162, no. 3859 (December 13, 1968): 1247.

25. Simon Kuznets, "Appendices," in *Seasonal Variations in Industry and Trade* (New York: National Bureau of Economic Research, 1933), https://www.nber.org/chapters/c2204.pdf.

2 WATER AND FAMINE

1. William Digby, *The Famine Campaign in Southern India*, 2 vols. (London: Longmans, Green, 1878), 1:70.

2. Digby, *Famine Campaign*, 1:69.

3. William Digby, *"Prosperous" British India: A Revelation from Official Records* (London: T. Fisher Unwin, 1901).

4. Tim Dyson, *A Population History of India: From the First Modern People to the Present Day* (Oxford: Oxford University Press, 2018), 158.

5. The Famine Commission of 1898 described the scale of construction of wells, which was large, but the enterprise suffered from high incidence of failed construction. India, *Report of the Indian Famine Commission, 1898* (Simla: Government Press, 1898), 185–186.

6. D. A. Mooley and B. Parthasarathy, "Fluctuations in All-India Summer Monsoon Rainfall during 1871–1978," *Climatic Change* 6 (September 1984): 287–301.

7. Hyderabad, *The Economic Life of Hyderabad* (Hyderabad: Government Press, 1937), 117.

8. Bombay, *Report on the Famine of the Bombay Presidency* (Bombay: Government Press, 1903), 8.

9. H. H. Mann, *Well Waters from the Trap Area of Western India* (Pune: Yeravada Prison Press, 1915), 3.

10. Paul Baumann, "The Dry Monsoon of the Deccan Plateau," available at http://employees.oneonta.edu/baumanpr/geosat2/Dry_Monsoon/Dry_Monsoon.htm.

11. India, *Report of the Indian Famine Commission*, pt. 1, *Famine Relief* (London: HMSO, 1880), 108.

12. India, *Papers regarding the Famine and the Relief Operations in India during 1900–1902*, vol. 1, *British Districts* (London: HMSO, 1902), 262.

13. India, *Papers regarding the Famine*, 1:263.

14. India, *Papers regarding the Famine*, 1:176.

15. India, *Papers regarding the Famine*, 1:263.

16. India, *Papers regarding the Famine*, 1:176.

17. Water security entered the discourse of famine response in western India before 1876, but the discourse was random in character. A framework of relief emerged in the last quarter of the century, and water occupied a central place in it in the later years. For a discussion of the water initiatives in early nineteenth-century famines, see George Adamson, "'The Most Horrible of Evils': Social Responses to Drought and Famine in the Bombay Presidency, 1782–1857," in *Natural Hazards and Peoples in the Indian Ocean World*, ed. Greg Bankoff and Joseph Christensen (Basingstoke: Palgrave, 2016), 79–104.

18. The 1899 famine "was a famine of water as well as of food." India, *Report of the Indian Famine Commission, 1901* (Calcutta: Government Press, 1901), 61.

19. "The Famine in India: Nasik District," *Times of India*, February 20, 1900, 4.

20. Baroda, *Report of Famine Operations in the Baroda State 1911–12* (Bombay: Times of India Press, 1913), 22.

21. Arup Maharatna, *The Demography of Famines: An Indian Historical Perspective* (Delhi: Oxford University Press, 1996).

22. India, *Report of the Indian Famine Commission* (1880), pt. 1, 28.

23. India, *Papers regarding the Famine*, 1:33.

24. India, *Papers regarding the Famine*, 1:367.

25. India. *Appendix to the Report of the Indian Famine Commission, 1898, Being Minutes of Evidence, Etc.*, vol. 1, *Bengal* (London: HMSO, 1898), 112.

26. India, *Papers regarding the Famine*, 1:28.

27. India, *Papers regarding the Famine*, 1:38, 140.

28. India, *Report of the Indian Famine Commission, 1901*, 61.

29. Bombay, *Report of the Famine in the Bombay Presidency in 1896–97* (Bombay: Government Press, 1898), xcix.

30. Bombay, *Famine Relief Code: Bombay Presidency* (Pune: Yeravada Prison Press, 1927), 42.

31. India, *Report of the Indian Famine Commission* (1880), pt. 1, 108.

32. *Quarterly Journal of the Poona Sarvajanik Sabha*, ed. S. H. Chiplonkar, 1878, 7.

33. India, *Papers regarding the Famine*, 1:238.

34. "Even in non-famine times, social discrimination against low-caste and Untouchable labourers often obliged them to drink from readily contaminated water sources." David Arnold, "Cholera and Colonialism in British India," *Past and Present* 113 (November 1986): 126. The citation refers to a 1951 epidemiological study of cholera in the Madras Presidency.

35. India, *Report of the Indian Famine Commission, 1901*, 61. "Orders were also issued granting certain concessions to owners of private wells who allowed the public to draw water for domestic consumption, and wherever people of low caste were to be supplied from these wells, Government undertook the expenditure of providing special water carriers." Bombay, *Report on the Famine*, 42.

36. India, *Papers regarding the Famine*, 1:262.

37. I emphasize that the type of events of interest here is the dryland famine. Two events dominate the historiography of famines in India, in 1770 and 1943. Both occurred in Bengal. Although natural disasters and crop failure did precede both episodes, Bengal is a relatively water-rich area. Most parts of this large area are not arid. The attention of famine scholars, therefore, fell on "human-made" causes such as the indifference of the European rulers of these regions, warfare, and a failure of the regional state. The exact combination of factors that caused these two famines remains debated. Preoccupation with these two events might make us lose sight of the geographical agency behind disasters in the semiarid areas where famines were more frequent than in Bengal. The historical scholarship suffers from that oversight.

38. The number of times the words *railways* and *food* were mentioned in the three Famine Commission reports covering the Deccan famines

fell steadily, and the number of times *cholera* was mentioned rose—suggesting a shift of accent from food distribution to water quality in the famine relief paradigm. See Tirthankar Roy, "Water, Climate, and Economy in India from 1880 to the Present," *Journal of Interdisciplinary History* 51, no. 4 (Spring 2021): 565–594. Arnold, "Cholera and Colonialism," discusses the "synchronization" of famine and cholera in the late nineteenth century.

39. Madras, *Report of the Water-Supply and Drainage Committee* (Madras: Government Press, 1947), 22.

40. Histories of pre-British famines ignore the problem, for example, H. H. Khondker, "Famine Policies in Pre-British India and the Question of Moral Economy," *South Asia: Journal of South Asian Studies* 9, no. 1 (1986): 25–40, which Mike Davis cites to make the doubtful and unverifiable claim that precolonial India practiced "humanitarian . . . traditions of dignified relief." Mike Davis, *Late Victorian Holocausts: El Niño Famines and the Making of the Third World* (London: Verso, 2001), 167.

41. India, *Report of the Indian Famine Commission* (1880), pt. 1, 5.

42. Michelle B. McAlpin, *Subject to Famine: Food Crisis and Economic Change in Western India, 1860–1920* (Princeton, NJ: Princeton University Press, 1983); Robin Burgess and Dave Donaldson, "Can Openness Mitigate the Effects of Weather Shocks? Evidence from India's Famine Era," *American Economic Review* 100, no. 2 (May 2010): 449–453.

43. India, *Report of the Indian Famine Commission* (1880), pt. 1, 18.

44. India, *Report of the Indian Famine Commission*, 52.

45. Edward Said, *Culture and Imperialism* (New York: Vintage, 1993), 9.

3 WATER AND EQUALITY

B. R. Ambedkar, "Gandhi and His Fast" (1932), in *Writings and Speeches* (New Delhi: Government Press, 1989), 5:373, emphasis added.

1. Tripta Wahi, "Rights to Sink and Repair Wells and Accruing Rights in Land and Its Produce," *Proceedings of the Indian History Congress* 72 (December 2011): 378–391.

2. B. R. Ambedkar, *Annihilation of Caste* (Bombay: B. R. Kadrekar, 1936).

3. P. V. Kane, *History of the Dharmasastra* (Pune: Bhandarkar Oriental Research Institute, 1930–1962), vol. 2, pt. 1 (1941), 23.

4. "A reservoir of water belonging to Chándálas is serviceable only to Chándálas, but not to others." Kautilya, *Arthashastra*, trans. R. Shama Sastri (Bangalore: Government Press, 1915), 29. See also Deepa Joshi and Ben Fawcett, "Water, Hindu Mythology and an Unequal Social Order in India" (paper presented at the Second Conference of the International Water History Association, Bergen, Norway, 2011).

5. See, for example, R. V. Russell and Hira Lal, *Tribes and Castes of the Central Provinces* (Nagpur: Government Press, 1915).

6. Louis Dumont, *Homo Hierarchicus: The Caste System and Its Implications* (Chicago: University of Chicago Press, 1970), 43.

7. Leif Wenar, "The Nature of Rights," *Philosophy and Public Affairs* 33 (2005): 223–252, reprinted in *Rights: Concepts and Contexts*, ed. Brian H. Bix and Horacio Spector (Abingdon: Routledge, 2016), 213–242.

8. Ambedkar, "Gandhi and His Fast," 373, emphasis added.

9. Mike Davis, *Late Victorian Holocausts: El Niño Famines and the Making of the Third World* (London: Verso, 2001), 331, emphasis added.

10. David Ludden, "Orientalist Empiricism: Transformations of Colonial Knowledge," in *Orientalism and the Postcolonial Predicament: Perspectives on South Asia*, ed. Carol A. Breckenridge and Peter van der Veer (Philadelphia: University of Pennsylvania Press, 1993), 250–278; Nicholas B. Dirks, *Castes of Mind: Colonialism and the Making of Modern India* (Princeton, NJ: Princeton University Press, 2001); Burton Stein, *Thomas Munro: The Origins of the Colonial State and His Vision of Empire* (Delhi: Oxford University Press, 1989).

11. For example, Bernard Cohn, a mentor to the scholarship: "Vast amounts of knowledge were transformed into textual forms [and] deployed by the colonial state in fixing, bounding, and settling India." Bernard Cohn, *Colonialism and Its Forms of Knowledge: The British in India* (Princeton, NJ: Princeton University Press, 1997), 8. Dirks, *Castes of Mind*, makes a fuller statement of transformed traditions.

12. David Mosse, "Colonial and Contemporary Ideologies of 'Community Management': The Case of Tank Irrigation Development in South India," *Modern Asian Studies* 33, no. 2 (May 1999): 303–338.

13. "The Depressed Classes welcomed the British," Ambedkar said, "as their deliverers from age long tyranny and oppression by the

orthodox Hindus." B. R. Ambedkar, speech at the Round Table Conference, 1930, in Ambedkar, *Writings and Speeches*, 2 (New Delhi: Government Press, 1982), 504.

14. Damodar Dharmananda Kosambi, *The Culture and Civilisation of Ancient India in Historical Outline* (London: Routledge and Kegan Paul, 1965), 88.

15. Mihir Shah, "Structures of Power in India Society: A Response," *Economic and Political Weekly*, 43, no. 46 (November 15, 2008): 79.

16. For a critique of the myth of an "eco-golden age" in water access in rural India, see Shri Krishan, "Water Harvesting Traditions and the Social Milieu in India: A Second Look," *Economic and Political Weekly* 46, nos. 26–27 (June 25, 2011): 87–95.

17. "Appellate Side: Defilement of Well Water," *Times of India*, July 28, 1914.

18. "Caste Warfare," *Times of India*, August 16, 1924.

19. "Water, Water!," *Times of India*, April 25, 1925.

20. "Untouchables Use Water from Common Pond," *Times of India*, November 21, 1931.

21. "Untouchables Win: Mahad Tank Declared Public Property," *Times of India*, January 22, 1931.

22. For descriptions of the Mahad incident and its legacy, see Gail Omvedt, *Dalit Visions: The Anti-caste Movement and the Construction of an Indian Identity* (Hyderabad: Orient Longman, 2006), 44; and Anupama Rao, *The Caste Question: Dalits and the Politics of Modern India* (Berkeley: University of California Press, 2009).

23. For some examples of a non-Brahmin movement, see Adapa Satyanarayana, "Nation, Caste, and the Past: Articulation of Dalitbahujan Identity, Consciousness and Ideology," *Proceedings of the Indian History Congress* 65 (2004): 416–467.

24. For one such case involving the Arya Samaj, see Kenneth W. Jones, "Ham Hindu Nahin: Arya-Sikh Relations, 1877–1905," *Journal of Asian Studies* 32, no. 3 (May 1973): 457–475.

25. "Whipped for Using Public Tank: Mr. Gandhi's Allegation," *Times of India*, November 6, 1933, 5.

26. "Fight over Village Well: Harijans versus Caste Hindus," *Times of India*, March 2, 1934, 6.

27. "Hindu-Harijan Clash in Mysore," *Times of India*, March 29, 1935, 12.

28. "Nasik Campaign Called Off," *Times of India*, December 17, 1935, 6.

29. "Tense Situation in Bijnor: Use of Wells by Harijans," *Times of India*, September 9, 1938, 15.

30. "Social Boycott in C.P. Village: Harijan Woman's Use of a Public Well," *Times of India*, April 27, 1934, 3.

31. "Water Supply in Presidency: Bombay Govt. Grants," *Times of India*, October 31, 1930, 11.

32. M. G. Bhagat, "The Untouchable Classes of Maharashtra," *Journal of the University of Bombay* 4, pt. 1 (July 1935): 163.

33. "Bombay Suburban Wells Dispute: Tension Growing," *Times of India*, February 4, 1933, 18.

34. Rao, *Caste Question*, 80.

35. "The Depressed Classes: Progress in Western India," *Times of India*, November 24, 1932.

36. "Great Scarcity of Water at Poona," *Times of India*, June 4, 1872, 3.

37. Thomas Blaney, "Our Inefficient Water-Supply," letter to the editor, *Times of India*, May 5, 1884, 6.

38. D. Arulanandam Pillai, "Problems relating to Paraiyas in the Tanjore District," in *Papers Read at the Third Annual Conference of the Indian Economic Association Held in the Senate House, Madras, 1919–1920* (Madras: Indian Economic Association, 1920), 88.

39. India, *Papers relating to Village Sanitation in India, 1888–1895* (Calcutta: Government Press, 1896), 8.

40. India, *Papers relating to Village Sanitation*, 10.

41. "Use of Public Wells by Depressed Classes: Bombay Government's Resolution," *Times of India*, February 10, 1933, 10.

42. A. V. Raman Rao, *Structure and Working of Village Panchayats* (Pune: Gokhale Institute of Politics and Economics, 1954), 15.

43. Raman Rao, *Village Panchayats*, 15.

44. Madras, *Report of the Water-Supply and Drainage Committee* (Madras: Government Press, 1947), 9.

45. I. P. Desai, *Water Facilities for the Untouchables in Rural Gujarat: A Report* (New Delhi: Indian Council of Social Science Research, 1973).

46. Cited in Sukhadeo Thorat, "Oppression and Denial: Dalit Discrimination in the 1990s," *Economic and Political Weekly* 37, no. 6 (February 9, 2002): 572–578.

47. Thorat, "Oppression and Denial." On persistence of water discrimination, see also Hannah Johns, "Stigmatization of Dalits in Access to Water and Sanitation in India" (National Campaign on Dalit Human Rights, New Delhi, ca. 2012).

48. Sanjiv J. Phansalkar, "Water, Equity and Development," *International Journal of Rural Management* 3, no. 1 (January 2007): 1–25.

49. Thorat, "Oppression and Denial," 575.

50. Mukul Sharma, *Caste and Nature: Dalits and Indian Environmental Politics* (Delhi: Oxford University Press, 2017), 183.

51. Exclusion persists, sometimes in invisible ways. For example, a doctoral study of women's rights to the commons in Tamil Nadu finds an instance where a village council "failed to disclose" that a water body it maintained was accessible to all. Jayshree Priyadarshani Mangubhai, "Human Rights as Practice: Dalit Women's Collective Action to Secure Livelihood Entitlements in Rural South India" (PhD diss., University of Utrecht, 2012), 74.

52. A. M. Shah, "Purity, Impurity, Untouchability: Then and Now," *Sociological Bulletin* 56, no. 3 (September 2007): 355–368.

4 BECOMING A PUBLIC GOOD

1. David Gilmartin, "Scientific Empire and Imperial Science: Colonialism and Irrigation Technology in the Indus Basin," *Journal of Asian Studies* 53, no. 4 (November 1994): 1127–1149.

2. Aparajith Ramnath, *The Birth of an Indian Profession: Engineers, Industry, and the State, 1900–47* (New Delhi: Oxford University Press, 2017).

3. Bombay, *Report on a Project for the Supply of Water to the Poona Cantonment* (Bombay: Education Society's Press, 1858).

4. "The Romance of Mairwara," *Blackwood's Edinburgh Magazine*, February 1853, 207–215; Charles George Dixon, *Sketch of Mairwara* (London: Smith, Elder, 1850).

5. G. Gordon, "On the Value of Water, and Its Storage and Distribution in Southern India," *Minutes of Proceedings of the Institution of Civil Engineers* 33, 1872, 376–400.

6. Sadhu Singh Ahluwalia, "The Economic Condition of the Sikhs" (PhD thesis, Gokhale Institute of Politics and Economics, Pune, 1959), pt. 1, 188–189.

7. Ahluwalia, "Economic Condition of the Sikhs," pt. 1, 297.

8. R. MacLagan Gorrie, "Soil and Water Conservation in the Punjab," *Geographical Review* 28, no. 1 (January 1938): 30.

9. Margaret R. Biswas and Asit K. Biswas, "Complementarity between Environment and Development Processes," *Environmental Conservation* 11, no. 1 (August 1984): 35.

10. Lloyd I. Rudolph and Susanne Hoeber Rudolph, *In Pursuit of Lakshmi: The Political Economy of the Indian State* (Chicago: University of Chicago Press, 1987), 54.

11. Minoti Chakravarty-Kaul, *Common Lands and Customary Law: Institutional Change in North India over the Past Two Centuries* (Delhi: Oxford University Press, 1996).

12. J. V. Woodman, *A Digest of Indian Law Cases: Containing High Court Reports, 1862–1900* (Calcutta: Government Press, 1901), 927, 1037.

13. In 1974, an appeals case, *Narsoo v. Madan Lal and others* (Madhya Pradesh High Court), decided whether flowing rainwater could be deemed a "stream" involving customary or easement right, or not, in which case, any landowner able to do so could impound the water.

14. Videh Upadhyay, "The Ownership of Water in Indian Laws," in *Water and the Laws in India*, ed. Ramaswamy R. Iyer (New Delhi: Sage, 2009), 135.

15. Some early work on the nature of the right anticipates the main issues in the later scholarship. See Chhatrapati Singh, *Water Rights and Principles of Water Resources Management* (Bombay: N. M. Tripathi, 1991).

16. Ramaswamy R. Iyer, introduction to *Water and the Laws in India*, ed. Ramaswamy R. Iyer (New Delhi: Sage, 2009), xi–xiv.

17. Joseph L. Sax, "The Public Trust Doctrine in Natural Resource Law: Effective Judicial Intervention," *Michigan Law Review* 68, no. 3 (1970): 485.

18. Jona Razzaque, "Application of Public Trust Doctrine in Indian Environmental Cases," *Journal of Environmental Law* 13, no. 2 (September 2001): 221–234.

19. Philippe Cullet, *Water Law, Poverty, and Development: Water Sector Reforms in India* (Oxford: Oxford University Press, 2009), 47–49.

20. Aviram Sharma, "Drinking Water Quality in Indian Water Policies, Laws, and Courtrooms: Understanding the Intersections of Science and Law in Developing Countries," *Bulletin of Science, Technology and Society* 37, no. 1 (February 2017): 45–56.

21. P. B. Anand, "Right to Water and Access to Water: An Assessment," *Journal of International Development* 19, no. 4 (2007): 511–526.

22. Erin L. O'Donnell and Julia Talbot-Jones, "Creating Legal Rights for Rivers: Lessons from Australia, New Zealand, and India," *Ecology and Society* 23, no. 1 (March 2018), https://doi.org/10.5751/ES-09854-230107.

23. Christopher D. Stone, "Should Trees Have Standing? Toward Legal Rights for Natural Objects," *Southern California Law Review* 45 (1972): 488–489.

24. Kelly D. Alley, "River Goddesses, Personhood and Rights of Nature: Implications for Spiritual Ecology," *Religions* 10, no. 9 (2019), https://www.mdpi.com/2077-1444/10/9/502.

25. Sridhar Rengarajan, Dhivya Palaniyappan, Purvaja Ramachandran, and Ramesh Ramachandran, "National Green Tribunal of India—an Observation from Environmental Judgements," *Environmental Science and Pollution Research* 25, no. 12 (April 2018): 11313–11318.

5 WATER IN THE CITIES

1. Cuthbert Finch, "Vital Statistics of Calcutta," *Quarterly Journal of the Royal Statistical Society of London* 13 (May 1850): 179.

2. For the population data, see Tirthankar Roy, *An Economic History of India, 1707–1857* (Abingdon: Routledge, 2021).

3. Tirthankar Roy, *The Economic History of India, 1857–2010*, 4th ed. (Delhi: Oxford University Press, 2020).

4. John Broich, "Engineering the Empire: British Water Supply Systems and Colonial Societies, 1850–1900," *Journal of British Studies* 46, no. 2 (April 2007): 365.

5. Mariam Dossal, "Henry Conybeare and the Politics of Centralised Water Supply in Mid-Nineteenth Century Bombay," *Indian Economic and Social History Review* 25, no. 1 (March 1988): 79–96; Sapana Doshi,

"Imperial Water, Urban Crisis: A Political Ecology of Colonial State Formation in Bombay, 1850–1890," *Review (Fernand Braudel Center)* 37, nos. 3–4 (2014): 173–218.

6. Dinshaw E. Wacha, *Rise and Growth of Bombay Municipal Government* (Madras: G. A. Natesan, 1913), 99.

7. Wacha, *Bombay Municipal Government*, 106.

8. Ira Klein, "Urban Development and Death: Bombay City, 1870–1914," *Modern Asian Studies* 20, no. 4 (October 1986): 730.

9. A presidency was a large administrative division in British India.

10. Klein, "Urban Development and Death," 754.

11. "Water for Bombay," *Economic and Political Weekly* 2, no. 21 (May 27, 1967): 947–948.

12. Bombay, *Report of the Local Self-Government Committee* (Bombay: Government Press, 1940), 97.

13. Cited in "The Water-Supply of Calcutta," *British Medical Journal* 1, no. 481 (March 19, 1870): 293.

14. "The Water Supply and the Health of Calcutta," *British Medical Journal* 1, no. 1733 (March 17, 1894): 596.

15. "India: Reports from Calcutta; Water Supply of Calcutta; Plague and Cholera," *Public Health Reports (1896–1970* 18, no. 49 (December 4, 1903): 2164.

16. "Water Supply of Calcutta; Plague and Cholera," 2163.

17. "Madras Water," *British Medical Journal* 2, no. 359 (November 16, 1867): 456.

18. "Madras Water."

19. Susan J. Lewandowski, "Urban Growth and Municipal Development in the Colonial City of Madras, 1860–1900," *Journal of Asian Studies* 34, no. 2 (February 1975): 341–360.

20. S. M. Edwardes, comp., *A Memoir of Rao Bahadur Ranchhodlal Chhotalal* (Exeter, UK: W. Pollard, 1920). See also Howard Spodek, "City Planning in India under British Rule," *Economic and Political Weekly* 48, no. 4 (January 26, 2013): 53–61.

21. Mattia Celio, Christopher A. Scott, and Mark Giordano, "Urban–Agricultural Water Appropriation: The Hyderabad, India Case," *Geographical Journal* 176, no. 1 (March 2010): 39–57.

22. D. R. Gadgil, *Poona: A Socio-economic Survey* (Pune: Gokhale Institute of Politics and Economics, 1952), pt. 2; Sulabha Brahme and Prakash Gole, *Deluge in Poona: Aftermath and Rehabilitation* (Pune: Gokhale Institute of Politics and Economics, 1967).

23. Gadgil, *Poona*, pt. 2, 235.

24. Hyderabad, *The Economic Life of Hyderabad* (Hyderabad: Government Press, 1930), 146.

25. India, *Report on National Water Supply and Sanitation Schemes* (New Delhi: Government Press, 1961), 3.

26. Kenneth A. MacKichan, "Estimated Use of Water in the United States—1950," U.S. Geological Survey, https://pubs.usgs.gov/circ/1951/circ115/htdocs/text.html.

27. Gadgil, *Poona*, pt. 2, 235.

28. India, *Report on National Water Supply*, 9.

29. Mrs. Whitehead, "Welfare Work in Madras City," in *Papers Read at the Third Annual Conference of the Indian Economic Association Held in the Senate House, Madras, 1919–1920* (Madras: Indian Economic Association, 1920), 43.

30. Anthony Acciavatti, "Re-imagining the Indian Underground: A Biography of the Tubewell," in *Places of Nature in Ecologies of Urbanism*, ed. Anne Rademacher and K. Sivaramakrishnan (Hong Kong: University of Hong Kong Press, 2017), 206–237.

31. Om Prakash Mathur et al., *State of the Cities: India* (New Delhi: Institute of Social Sciences, 2021).

32. Nikhil Anand, "Multiplicity: Water, Rules, and the Making of Connections in Mumbai," in *Governing Access to Essential Resources*, ed. Katharina Pistor and Olivier De Schutter (New York: Columbia University Press, 2016), 121.

33. Sharmila L. Murthy, "Land Security and the Challenges of Realizing the Human Right to Water and Sanitation in the Slums of Mumbai, India," *Health and Human Rights* 14, no. 2 (December 2012): 69.

34. Jayaraj Sundaresan, "Planning as Commoning: Transformation of a Bangalore Lake," *Economic and Political Weekly* 46, no. 50 (December 10, 2011): 71–79.

35. M. Gandy, "Rethinking Urban Metabolism: Water, Space and the Modern City," *City* 8, no. 3 (2004): 363–379.

36. Karen Coelho and Nithya V. Raman, "From the Frying Pan to the Floodplain: Negotiating Land, Water, and Fire in Chennai's Development," in *Ecologies of Urbanism in India: Metropolitan Civility and Sustainability*, ed. Anne Rademacher and K. Sivaramakrishnan (Hong Kong: Hong Kong University Press, 2013), 145–168.

37. Tushaar Shah and Barbara van Koppen, "Is India Ripe for Integrated Water Resources Management? Fitting Water Policy to National Development Context," *Economic and Political Weekly* 41, no. 31 (August 5, 2006): 3416.

6 WATER STRESS

1. Parliamentary debates, March 30, 1951, https://eparlib.nic.in/bit stream/123456789/760406/1/ppd_30-03-1951.pdf.

2. Velayutham Saravanan, *Water and the Environmental History of Modern India* (London: Bloomsbury, 2020).

3. Elizabeth Whitcombe, *Agrarian Conditions in Northern India* (Berkeley: University of California Press, 1972), vol. 1; Indu Agnihotri, "Ecology, Land Use and Colonisation: The Canal Colonies of Punjab," *Indian Economic and Social History Review* 33, no. 1 (March 1996): 59–68.

4. India, *Royal Commission on Agriculture*, vol. 7, *Evidence Taken in the United Provinces* (Delhi: Government Press, 1927), 377–379.

5. A pioneering effort to create an ecological map of India for 1930 revealed patterns of water stress in well-dependent dry regions in the Deccan and Gujarat. Daniel Thorner and Chen Han Seng, *Ecological and Agrarian Regions of South Asia circa 1930* (Karachi: Oxford University Press, 1996).

6. For a contemporary discussion, see Radhakamal Mukerjee, *The Rural Economy of India* (London: Longmans, Green, 1926).

7. Tirthankar Roy, "Roots of Agrarian Crisis in Interwar India: Retrieving a Narrative," *Economic and Political Weekly* 41, no. 52 (December 30, 2007): 5389–5400.

8. Satyajit Singh, "Evaluating Large Dams in India," *Economic and Political Weekly* 25, no. 11 (March 17, 1990): 561–574. For a short historical account of the river projects and the controversies around them, see Michael H. Fisher, *An Environmental History of India: From*

Earliest Times to the Twenty-First Century (Cambridge: Cambridge University Press, 2018).

9. Ashok K. Mitra, "Underutilisation Revisited: Surface Irrigation in Drought Prone Areas of Western Maharashtra," *Economic and Political Weekly* 21, no. 17 (April 26, 1986): 752–756. On the problem in the Krishna basin, the largest field of irrigation development in the Deccan plateau, see Bret Wallach, "Irrigation Developments in the Krishna Basin since 1947," *Geographical Review* 74, no. 2 (April 1984): 127–144.

10. "The rules are resources that are called upon when needed." Peter Mollinga, *On the Waterfront: Water Distribution, Technology and Agrarian Change in a South Indian Canal Irrigation System* (Hyderabad: Orient Longman, 2003), 181.

11. Ashok K. Mitra, "Joint Management of Irrigation Systems in India: Relevance of Japanese Experience," *Economic and Political Weekly* 27, no. 26 (June 27, 1992): A75–A82.

12. Several examples of disputes over river water and attempts at resolving these are discussed in Madhav Gadgil and Ramachandra Guha, *Ecology and Equity: The Use and Abuse of Nature in Contemporary India* (London: Routledge, 1995), 76–81; and Saravanan, *Water*.

13. Robert H. Wade, "Muddy Waters: Inside the World Bank as It Struggled with the Narmada Projects," *Economic and Political Weekly* 46, no. 40 (October 1, 2011): 44–65.

14. For a discussion of distributional conflicts, and a case study, see Saravanan, *Water*.

15. Brahma Chellaney, *Water: Asia's New Battleground* (Washington, DC: Georgetown University Press, 2011).

16. Paula Hanasz, "Power Flows: Hydro-Hegemony and Water Conflicts in South Asia," *Security Challenges* 10, no. 3 (2014): 95–112.

17. On the Indus treaty, see Ramaswamy R. Iyer, "Indus Waters Treaty 1960: An Indian Perspective," Heinrich Böll Stiftung, March 16, 2014, https://www.boell.de/en/2014/03/16/indus-waters-treaty-1960-indian-perspective. On the eastern borders, India's decision to build a barrage on the Ganges on the Bangladesh border (1973–1974) caused much uneasiness between the two countries. Comparatively speaking, river-sharing arrangements between India and Nepal and between India and Bhutan were more peaceful.

18. Daanish Mustafa, "Social Construction of Hydropolitics: The Geographical Scales of Water and Security in the Indus Basin," *Geographical Review* 97, no. 4 (2007): 484.

19. Mustafa, "Social Construction of Hydropolitics," 497.

20. G. Samba Siva Reddy, "Making of Micro-Regional Identities in the Colonial Context: Studying the Rayalaseema Maha Sabha, 1934–1956," *Proceedings of the Indian History Congress* 67 (2006–2007): 500–513; Bethany Lacina, *Rival Claims: Ethnic Violence and Territorial Autonomy under Indian Federalism* (Ann Arbor: University of Michigan Press, 2017), 71.

21. Paul Singh Dhillon, *Water Resources Development and Management in North-West India: Some Issues* (Chandigarh: Centre for Research in Rural and Industrial Development, 1987).

22. Sailen Routray, Patrik Oskarsson, and Puspanjali Satpathy, "A Hydrologically Fractured State? Nation-Building, the Hirakud Dam and Societal Divisions in Eastern India," *South Asia: Journal of South Asian Studies* 43, no. 3 (2020): 429–445.

23. India, *Symposium on Integrated Development of Surface and Subsurface Water Resources* (New Delhi: Government Press, 1971), vol. 1.

24. Rajni Jain, Prabhat Kishore, and Dhirendra Kumar Singh, "Irrigation in India: Status, Challenges and Options," *Journal of Soil and Water Conservation* 18, no. 4 (2019): 354–363.

25. Himanshu Kulkarni and Mihir Shah, "Punjab Water Syndrome: Diagnostics and Prescriptions," *Economic and Political Weekly* 48, no. 52 (December 28, 2013): 72.

26. Navroz K. Dubash, "The Electricity-Groundwater Conundrum: Case for a Political Solution to a Political Problem," *Economic and Political Weekly* 42, no. 52 (December 29, 2007–January 4, 2008): 45–55.

27. Bharat Punjabi and Craig A. Johnson, "The Politics of Rural–Urban Water Conflict in India: Untapping the Power of Institutional Reform," *World Development* 120 (August 2019): 182.

28. Mattia Celio, Christopher A. Scott, and Mark Giordano, "Urban–Agricultural Water Appropriation: The Hyderabad, India Case," *Geographical Journal* 176, no. 1 (March 2010): 39–57.

29. Tushaar Shah and Shilp Verma, "Addressing Water Management," in *Getting India Back on Track: An Action Agenda for Reform*, ed.

Bibek Debroy, Ashley J. Tellis, and Reece Trevor (Washington, DC: Carnegie Endowment for International Peace, 2014), 189.

30. P. S. Vijay Shankar, Himanshu Kulkarni, and Sunderrajan Krishnan, "India's Groundwater Challenge and the Way Forward," *Economic and Political Weekly* 46, no. 2 (January 8, 2011): 37–45.

31. Marcus Moench, "Drawing Down the Buffer: Science and Politics of Ground Water Management in India," *Economic and Political Weekly* 27, no. 13 (March 28, 1992): A7–A14.

32. Jean-Philippe Venot, Bharat R. Sharma, and K. V. G. K. Rao, "Krishna Basin Development: Interventions to Limit Downstream Environmental Degradation," *Journal of Environment and Development* 17, no. 3 (September 2008): 269–291.

33. Tushaar Shah, *Ground Water Markets and Irrigation Development: Political Economy and Practical Policy* (Bombay: Oxford University Press, 1993).

34. Siwan Anderson, "Caste as an Impediment to Trade," *American Economic Journal: Applied Economics* 3, no. 1 (January 2011): 261.

35. Cited in C. H. Hanumantha Rao, "Sustainable Use of Water for Irrigation in Indian Agriculture," *Economic and Political Weekly* 37, no. 18 (May 4, 2002): 1744.

36. S. Janakarajan and Marcus Moench, "Are Wells a Potential Threat to Farmers' Well-Being? Case of Deteriorating Groundwater Irrigation in Tamil Nadu," *Economic and Political Weekly* 41, no. 37 (September 16, 2006): 3986.

37. Interlocking means that two or more markets (land, credit, water) share a common seller. An easier tenancy term, then, could balance against a high interest rate or water rate.

38. Amalendu Jyotishi and Satyapriya Rout, "Water Rights in Deccan Region: Insights from Baliraja and Other Water Institutions," *Economic and Political Weekly* 40, no. 2 (January 8, 2005): 155.

39. Manish K. Thakur and Binay K. Pattnaik, "How Effective Are 'Pani Panchayats'? A Fieldview from Maharashtra," *Sociological Bulletin* 51, no. 2 (September 2002): 243–268.

40. N. C. Narayanan and Lalitha Kamath, "Rural Water Access: Governance and Contestation in a Semi-Arid Watershed in Udaipur, Rajasthan," *Economic and Political Weekly* 47, no. 4 (January 28, 2012): 71. See also the

critical reviews of the water councils of Odisha in Sushanta Mahapatra, "Functioning of Water Users Associations or Pani Panchayat in Orissa: Principle, Procedure, Performance and Prospects," *Law, Environment and Development Journal* 3, no. 2 (September 2007): 126–147; Basanta Kumar Sahu, "*Pani Panchayat* in Orissa, India: The Practice of Participatory Water Management," *Development* 51 (2008): 121–125; and Anjal Prakash and R. K. Sama, "Social Undercurrents in a Water-Scarce Village," *Economic and Political Weekly* 41, no. 7 (February 18, 2006): 577–579.

41. Mihir Shah, "Water: Towards a Paradigm Shift in the Twelfth Plan," *Economic and Political Weekly* 48, no. 3 (January 19, 2013): 44. An *ahar-pyne* is a network of channels and retention ponds; a *tanka* is a rainwater-harvesting tank; a *dhara* harvests natural spring water; *talabs* are human-made ponds; *eri* is another name for the tanks.

42. A. Narayanamoorthy, "Drip and Sprinkler Irrigation in India: Benefits, Potential and Future Directions" (draft prepared for the International Water Management Institute, Colombo, 2006).

43. C. S. Bahinipati and P. K. Viswanathan, "Can Micro-Irrigation Technologies Resolve India's Groundwater Crisis? Reflections from Dark-Regions in Gujarat," *International Journal of the Commons* 13, no. 2 (2019): 848–858.

44. A. Suresh, K. S. Aditya, Girish Jha, and Suresh Pal, "Micro-Irrigation Development in India: An Analysis of Distributional Pattern and Potential Correlates," *International Journal of Water Resources Development* 35, no. 6 (2019): 999–1014.

45. Philippe Cullet, "Model Groundwater (Sustainable Management) Bill, 2017: A New Paradigm for Groundwater Regulation," *Indian Law Review* 2, no. 3 (2017): 263–276.

46. Robert G. Wirsing, "Hydro-Politics in South Asia: The Domestic Roots of Interstate River Rivalry," *Asian Affairs: An American Review* 34 (2007): 3–22.

7 SEASONALITY

1. Rabindranath Tagore, "Big Sister," trans. Ketaki Kushari Dyson, in *I Won't Let You Go* (London: Bloodaxe Books, 2010), 104.

2. Dipesh Chakrabarty, *Rethinking Working-Class History: Bengal, 1890–1940* (Princeton, NJ: Princeton University Press, 1989), 11.

3. Cited in Ian J. Kerr, "On the Move: Circulating Labor in Pre-colonial, Colonial, and Post-colonial India," *International Review of Social History* 51, no. S14 (November 2006): 89.

4. Dirk H. A. Kolff, "Peasants Fighting for a Living in Early Modern North India," in *Fighting for a Living: A Comparative Study of Military Labour 1500–2000*, ed. Erik-Jan Zürcher (Amsterdam: Amsterdam University Press, 2013), 264.

5. Jim Corbett, *Man-Eaters of Kumaon* (Bombay: Oxford University Press, 1944), 24.

6. Jan Lucassen, "The Brickmakers' Strikes on the Ganges Canal in 1848–1849," *International Review of Social History* 51, no. S16 (September 2006): S47–83.

7. The Provincial Banking Enquiry Commission collected evidence from different provinces. The picture varied in detail from one region to the next, but the general features did not vary a lot.

8. Punjab, *The Punjab Provincial Banking Enquiry Committee 1929–30*, 2 vols. (Lahore: Government Press, 1930), 2:495.

9. India, *Royal Commission on Labour in India: Evidence*, vol. 2, pt. 1, *Punjab, Delhi (Provincial and Central) and Ajmer-Merwara* (London: HMSO, 1930), 150, emphasis added.

10. Douglas Haynes and Tirthankar Roy, "Conceiving Mobility: Weavers' Migrations in Pre-colonial and Colonial India," *Indian Economic and Social History Review* 36, no. 1 (1999): 35–67.

11. W. Arthur Lewis, "Economic Development with Unlimited Supplies of Labour," *The Manchester School* 22, no. 2 (May 1954), 139–191.

12. On the unusual low age at marriage in India and how that shaped women's work, see discussion in Tirthankar Roy, *The Economic History of India, 1857–2010*, 4th ed. (Delhi: Oxford University Press, 2020), 261–263.

13. An argument known as the land-abundance view of precolonial Africa suggests that an abundance of low-quality land and labor scarcity induced the emergence of labor coercion in precolonial Africa. Gareth Austin, "Cash Crops and Freedom: Export Agriculture and the Decline of Slavery in Colonial West Africa," *International Review of Social History* 54, no. 1 (April 2009): 1–37. The South India situation confirms the prediction somewhat.

14. India, *Census of India*, vol. 13, *Central Provinces and Berar* (Nagpur: Government Press, 1901), pt. 1, 213.

15. For an application to a later time, see P. Sanghvi, *Surplus Manpower in Agriculture and Economic Development, with Special Reference to India* (Bombay: Asia Publishing House, 1969).

16. Minding livestock was an important task. See M. Atchi Reddy, "Work and Leisure: Daily Working Hours of Agricultural Labourers, Nellore District, 1860–1989," *Indian Economic and Social History Review* 28, no. 1 (March 1991): 73–96.

17. India, *Census of India*, vol. 1, *Bombay Presidency* (Bombay: Government Press, 1881), 196.

18. Tirthankar Roy, *Rethinking Economic Change in India: Labour and Livelihood* (Abingdon: Routledge, 2005).

19. India, "National Commission on Agriculture" (extracts from the National Commission on Rural Labour), *Indian Journal of Labour Economics* 16 (1973): 65.

20. B. Gopalakrishna Hebbar and S. Bisaliah, "Stability in Seasonal Labour Absorption under Dryland Farming," *Artha Vijnana* 29, no. 3 (October 1987): 262–285.

21. Barbara Harriss-White, *India Working: Essays on Society and Economy* (Cambridge: Cambridge University Press, 2003), 19.

22. Priya Deshingkar and Daniel Start, "Seasonal Migration for Livelihoods in India: Coping, Accumulation and Exclusion," Working Paper 220 (Overseas Development Institute, London, 2003). See also Ben Rogaly, Jhuma Biswas, Daniel Coppard, Abdur Rafique, Kumar Rana, and Amrita Sengupta, "Seasonal Migration, Social Change and Migrants' Rights: Lessons from West Bengal," *Economic and Political Weekly* 36, no. 49 (December 8, 2001): 4547–4559.

23. Jan Breman, *Footloose Labour: Working in India's Informal Economy* (Cambridge: Cambridge University Press, 1996).

24. Prashant Bansode, "Seasonal Rural Migration: Quality of Life at Destination and Source; A Study of Sugarcane Cutter Migrants" (working paper, Gokhale Institute of Politics and Economics, Pune, 2014).

25. C. N. Cooke, *The Rise, Progress, and Present Condition of Banking in India* (Calcutta: Bengal Printing Company, 1863).

26. Marina Martin, "An Economic History of the Hundi, 1858–1978" (PhD diss., London School of Economics and Political Science, 2012).

27. Bengal, *Bengal Provincial Banking Enquiry Committee, 1929–30*, 3 vols. (Calcutta: Government Press, 1930), 3:165.

28. Bombay, *Report of the Bombay Provincial Banking Enquiry Committee, 1929–30*, 4 vols. (Bombay: Government Press, 1930), 1:196.

29. United Provinces, *Report of the United Provinces Provincial Banking Enquiry Committee*, 4 vols. (Allahabad: Government Press, 1930), 1:273.

30. Madras, *The Madras Provincial Banking Enquiry Committee*, 4 vols. (Madras: Government Press, 1930), 1:191.

31. Central Provinces and Berar, *Report of the Central Provinces Banking Enquiry Committee, 1929–30*, 4 vols. (Nagpur: Government Press, 1930), 4:933, 1:99.

32. Bengal, *Banking Enquiry Committee*, 3:93.

33. Madras, *Banking Enquiry Committee*, 4:289.

34. For example, B. R. Rau, *Present-Day Banking in India* (Calcutta: University of Calcutta, 1929), 3–4.

35. India, *The Indian Central Banking Enquiry Committee*, vol. 1, pt. 1, *Majority Report* (Calcutta: Government Press, 1931), 406.

36. Martin, "Economic History of the Hundi."

37. Central Provinces and Berar, *Banking Enquiry Committee*, 1:340.

38. The two most famous interventions were the Deccan Agriculturists Relief Act of 1879 and the Punjab Land Alienation Act of 1900. How serious the problem of land alienation was cannot be ascertained. The rate of land transfer tended to be low even without the laws. After the Indian Mutiny of 1857, officers were often unduly nervous about the prospect of peasant unrest. See Latika Chaudhary and Anand Swamy, "A Policy of Credit Disruption: The Punjab Land Alienation Act of 1900," *Economic History Review* 73, no. 1 (February 2020): 134–158; and Latika Chaudhary and Anand Swamy, "Protecting the Borrower: An Experiment in Colonial India," *Explorations in Economic History* 65, no. 3 (July 2017): 36–54.

39. Bengal, *Banking Enquiry Committee*, 3:93.

40. Bengal, *Banking Enquiry Committee*, 3:76–77.

41. United Provinces, *Banking Enquiry Committee*, 4:77.

42. See discussion in L. M. Bhole, *Financial Institutions and Markets: Structure, Growth and Innovations* (New Delhi: McGraw-Hill, 2004).

8 MONSOON ECONOMIES

1. Pandi Zdruli, Michael Cherlet, and Claudio Zucca, "Desertification: Mapping Constraints and Challenges," in *Encyclopedia of Soil Science*, ed. Rattan Lal, 3rd ed. (London: CRC Press, 2016), 1:633–641.

2. R. Meenu, S. Rehana, and P. P. Mujumdar, "Assessment of Hydrologic Impacts of Climate Change in Tunga–Bhadra River Basin, India with HEC-HMS and SDSM," *Hydrological Processes* 27, no. 11 (May 2013): 1572–1589; C. G. Madhusoodhanan, K. G. Sreeja, and T. I. Eldho, "Climate Change Impact Assessments on the Water Resources of India under Extensive Human Interventions," *Ambio* 45, no. 6 (October 2016): 725–741; Matthew Collins et al., "Long-Term Climate Change: Projections, Commitments and Irreversibility," in *Climate Change 2013: The Physical Science Basis; Contribution of Working Group I to the Fifth Assessment Report of the Intergovernmental Panel on Climate*, ed. T. F. Stocker et al. (Cambridge: Cambridge University Press, 2013), https://www.ipcc.ch/site/assets/uploads/2018/02/WG1AR5_Chapter12_FINAL.pdf, 1119 (on the monsoon).

3. Ram Fishman, "Groundwater Depletion Limits the Scope for Adaptation to Increased Rainfall Variability in India," *Climatic Change* 147, no. 1 (2018): 195–209.

4. Garrett Hardin, "Extensions of 'The Tragedy of the Commons,'" *Science* n.s. 280, no. 5364 (May 1998): 682.

SELECTED READINGS

This list contains works that I believe relate directly to the arguments of the book, including a few that were not cited in the text. It does not list sources I have drawn upon, or works with too specific an interest.

Agnihotri, Indu. "Ecology, Land Use and Colonisation: The Canal Colonies of Punjab." *Indian Economic and Social History Review* 33, no. 1 (March 1996): 59–68.

Amrith, Sunil. *Unruly Waters: How Mountain Rivers and Monsoons Have Shaped South Asia's History*. London: Penguin, 2018.

Broich, John. "Engineering the Empire: British Water Supply Systems and Colonial Societies, 1850–1900." *Journal of British Studies* 46, no. 2 (April 2007): 346–365.

Chellaney, Brahma. *Water: Asia's New Battleground*. Washington, DC: Georgetown University Press, 2011.

Christopher, Mark. *Water Wars: The Brahmaputra River and Sino-Indian Relations*. Newport, RI: US Naval War College, 2013.

Cullet, Philippe. *Water Law, Poverty, and Development: Water Sector Reforms in India*. Oxford: Oxford University Press, 2009.

Gallup, John Luke, Jeffrey D. Sachs, and Andrew D. Mellinger. "Geography and Economic Development." *International Regional Science Review* 22, no. 2 (1999): 179–123.

Hanasz, Paula. "Power Flows: Hydro-hegemony and Water Conflicts in South Asia." *Security Challenges* 10, no. 3 (2014): 95–112.

Hanumantha Rao, C. H. "Sustainable Use of Water for Irrigation in Indian Agriculture." *Economic and Political Weekly* 37, no. 18 (May 4, 2002): 1742–1745.

Hardin, Garrett. "Extensions of 'The Tragedy of the Commons.'" *Science* n.s. 280, no. 5364 (May 1988): 682–683.

India. *Indian Famine Commission, 1898*. Minutes of Evidence. Calcutta: Government Press, 1898.

India. *Report of the Indian Famine Commission, 1901*. Calcutta: Government Press, 1901.

Iyer, Ramaswamy R., ed. *Water and the Laws in India*. New Delhi: Sage, 2009.

Johns, Hannah. "Stigmatization of Dalits in Access to Water and Sanitation in India." National Campaign on Dalit Human Rights, New Delhi, ca. 2012.

Joshi, Deepa. "Caste, Gender and the Rhetoric of Reform in India's Drinking Water Sector." *Economic and Political Weekly* 46, no. 18 (2011): 56–63.

Mali, R. K., A. Gupta, R. Singh, and R. S. Singh. "Water Resource and Climate Change: An Indian Perspective." *Current Science* 90, no. 12 (2006): 1610–1626.

Mosse, David. *The Rule of Water: Statecraft, Ecology and Collective Action in South India*. Oxford: Oxford University Press, 2003.

Mustafa, Daanish. "Social Construction of Hydropolitics: The Geographical Scales of Water and Security in the Indus Basin." *Geographical Review* 97, no. 4 (2007): 484–501.

Omvedt, Gail. *Dalit Visions: The Anti-caste Movement and the Construction of an Indian Identity*. Hyderabad: Orient Longman, 2006.

Oshima, Harry T. *Economic Growth in Monsoon Asia: A Comparative Study*. Tokyo: University of Tokyo Press, 1987.

Punjabi, Bharat, and Craig A. Johnson. "The Politics of Rural–Urban Water Conflict in India: Untapping the Power of Institutional Reform." *World Development* 120 (August 2019): 182–192.

Rangarajan, Mahesh. "Environment and Ecology under British Rule." In *India and the British Empire*, edited by Douglas Peers and Nandini Gooptu, 212–230. Oxford: Oxford University Press, 2012.

Roy, Tirthankar. "Land Quality, Carrying Capacity, and Sustainable Agricultural Change in Twentieth-Century India." In *Economic Development and Environmental History in the Anthropocene: Perspectives on Asia and Africa*, edited by Gareth Austin, 159–178. London: Bloomsbury, 2017.

Roy, Tirthankar. "The Monsoon and the Market for Money in Late-Colonial India." *Enterprise and Society* 17, no. 2 (2016): 324–357.

Sachs, Jeffrey D. "Tropical Underdevelopment." Working paper. Center for International Development, Harvard University, Cambridge, MA, 2000.

Saravanan, Velayutham. *Water and the Environmental History of Modern India*. London: Bloomsbury, 2020.

Shah, Mihir, and P. S. Vijayshankar, eds. *Water: Growing Understanding, Emerging Perspectives*. Hyderabad: Orient Blackswan, 2016.

Shah, Tushaar, and Barbara van Koppen. "Is India Ripe for Integrated Water Resources Management? Fitting Water Policy to National Development Context." *Economic and Political Weekly* 41, no. 31 (August 5, 2006): 3413–3421.

Singh, Chhatrapati. *Water Rights and Principles of Water Resources Management*. Bombay: N. M. Tripathi, 1991.

Thorat, Sukhadeo. "Oppression and Denial: Dalit Discrimination in the 1990s." *Economic and Political Weekly* 37, no. 6 (February 9, 2002): 572–578.

Vijay Shankar, P. S., Himanshu Kulkarni, and Sunderrajan Krishnan. "India's Groundwater Challenge and the Way Forward." *Economic and Political Weekly* 46, no. 2 (January 8, 2011): 37–45.

INDEX

Adyar, 100
Agra, 124
Agriculture, 2, 4–6, 8, 11, 16, 23, 30, 41, 72, 90–91, 102, 117, 122, 128–129, 132–133, 135, 138, 147–149, 162, 164, 167–169
Ahmadabad, 101, 146, 162
Ajmer-Merwara, 69
Ambedkar, B. R., 45–49, 51, 53, 57, 62
Andhra Pradesh, 120, 133
Aqueducts, 68–69, 103
Aridity, 7, 9, 17, 21–22, 60, 170
Arkavathy, 104
Attached labor, 152

Baird Smith, Richard, 73
Bangalore, 104–105, 107–108, 110, 126
Banks, banking, 4, 17, 23, 91, 139, 154–159, 161–163, 165
Baroda, princely state, 54
Bartle Frere, Henry, 93–94
Beneficial enjoyment, 76
Bengal delta, 8, 17, 37, 115, 142

Bhakra dam, 74
Bhima, 29
Bihar, 132
Bombay (Mumbai), 17, 32, 52–53, 57–58, 62, 70, 87, 89, 92–97, 100–101, 102–103, 106–107, 109, 126–129, 146, 158, 160, 162
Bombay (province, region), 26, 31, 38–36, 56, 60
Bombay Backward Class Department, 56
Bombay Presidency, 95
Brahmaputra, 1
Braudel, Fernand, 20
Brickmaking, 71, 138, 142–143, 147, 150, 153
British empire, 3
British India. *See* Colonial India
Bundelkhand, 132
Burma, 160

Calcutta (Kolkata), 17, 87, 89, 97–100, 106–107, 138–139, 146, 158, 160, 162

Calcutta Waterworks Company, 97
Canals, 5–6, 26, 40–43, 66, 68, 70–77, 79, 92, 100, 114–118, 123, 127, 133–134, 142–143, 148
Capital market, 103, 154–164
Caravans, 140
Caste, 15, 20, 27, 35–36, 42, 44–63, 67, 73, 75, 80, 128–131, 150–151, 158, 159
Cautley, Proby, 71, 73
Census, 15, 150, 152
Chhattisgarh, 122
Chhotalal, Ranchhodlal, 101
China, 1, 18–19
Cholera, 34–38, 42–44, 87, 92, 99, 101
Cities, 7, 13, 16–17, 24, 30, 53, 56–59, 62, 66, 69, 85, 87–111, 122, 124, 126–128, 133, 135, 142, 148–149, 154, 157–158, 164
Coca-Cola, 82
Coleroon, 70
Colonial India, 6, 89, 92, 108, 114, 143, 150–151, 154
Colonialism, 3, 42, 44, 168, 174
Commons, 6, 22–23, 49–50, 65, 75–77, 80–82, 85, 109–110, 126, 129, 134, 174
Community development program, 60–61, 123
Constitution of India, 83
Construction industry, 133, 137–138, 140, 143, 148, 150, 153–154

Consumption, 4, 105–106, 133, 135, 146, 148–150, 155, 164, 168, 175
Conybeare, Henry, 70, 93
Cooum, 100
Cotton, Arthur, 70–71
Credit market. *See* Banks, banking; Capital market

Dalit, 48, 57, 62
Damodar, 115
Dams, 6, 11, 66, 68, 70, 75, 102, 114–117
Dasnami, 141
Deccan plateau, 26, 32, 37, 41, 46, 118, 132, 169
Deccan Traps, 26, 30, 124–125, 148
Development economics, 22
Digby, William, 25
District boards, 56
Dixon, C. G., 68–70
Drainage, 29, 38, 79, 87, 94, 96–97, 101, 111
Drips, 133–134, 175
Drought, 1, 4–5, 10, 15, 26–28, 31–36, 40, 43, 100, 103, 125, 129, 131–132, 159, 167
Dumont, Louis, 48–50

East India Company, 67, 71, 89–91, 99, 120, 141
Economic development, 74, 149
Economic history, 2, 13, 20–22, 24, 168, 171–173
El Niño Southern Oscillation, 27
Eminent domain, 78–79

Engineering, engineers, 68–73, 88, 92, 95, 104, 106, 116–117
Environmental history, 11, 21
Environmental Hygiene Committee, 1949, 105
Eradi, V. B., 113, 122
Europe, 3, 20–22, 37, 43, 106, 148, 168, 171–173

Factories, 5, 31, 91, 138–139, 147–148, 153–154, 164
Fairs, 146
Famine, 1, 4–5, 10–12, 14–15, 17, 23, 24–46, 49–51, 62, 66, 69, 71, 79, 81, 95, 100, 120, 123, 127, 138–140, 151, 168, 171–172
Famine Codes, 40
Famine Commissions, 25, 34, 36–37, 40, 45
Famine in Bengal, 1943, 5
Famine relief, 24, 27, 34, 36, 41–42, 44–45, 49, 100
Famines of 1876, 1896, 1898, 4, 26–27, 31–32, 36–37, 39–40, 42, 95, 103, 127
Farm servants, 151–152, 164
Fatehpur Sikri, 124
Fishing, 145
Floods, 4, 10–11, 12, 14, 111, 116, 159, 172
Flushing toilet, 103
Food production, 5, 16, 26, 40, 127
Fossil fuel, 2, 20, 68

Gandhi, M. K., 53, 55, 57
Ganges (Ganga), 71, 73, 84, 142–143
Gaur, 124
General labor, 152, 164
GeoSat, 31
Global warming, 1
Godavari, 29–31, 70, 102
Gold, 164–165
Great Indian Peninsula Railway, 32, 59
Green revolution, 67, 71, 75, 108, 121–123, 127–129

Hardin, Garrett, 22, 174
Haryana, 71, 121–122, 134
Himalayas, 17, 29, 40, 72–74, 114, 132, 142, 146, 170
Hirakud dam, 117
Hoeber, Susanne, 75
Hooghly, 97
Hundi, 158, 161
Hyderabad, city, 102, 104–105, 126
Hyderabad, princely state, 120

Imperial Bank, 156
Imperial Gazetteer (1909), 13
Indian Easements Act, 1882, 176
Indo-Gangetic Basin, 15, 40, 46, 75, 84, 114, 144, 148, 169
Inequality, 2, 4, 11, 14–15, 22, 36, 42–43, 49–51, 60, 66, 73, 75, 78, 87, 94, 105–106, 118, 127–129, 131, 164, 168, 171, 175
Influenza pandemic, 1918, 5, 28

Interest rate, 8, 17, 23, 139, 155–156, 159–160, 162–163
Interstate River Water Disputes Act, 1956, 120
Irrigation, 5, 14–15, 26–27, 31, 40, 42, 61, 68, 72–73, 75, 78–79, 85, 111, 114–116, 118, 123, 126–127, 130–132, 135, 144, 154, 172, 175
Irrigation Commissions, 40

Jamuna, 1
Jumna (Yamuna), 71, 73, 84, 142

Kane, P. V., 47
Karnataka, 30, 32, 53, 61, 118, 121, 133
Kashmir, 74
Kaveri, 31, 70, 104, 120–122
Kaveri waters dispute, 120
Kerala, 8, 17, 82
Köppen-Geiger, 6
Kosambi, D. D., 51
Krishna, 29–31, 70, 102, 128, 131
Kuznets, Simon, 23

Lakes, 13–14, 25, 30, 67, 70, 72, 79, 81, 88, 92–93, 100, 102, 104, 170
Land Degradation Assessment in Drylands, 169
Legislature, 46, 54, 56–57, 59, 63
Lewis, W. Arthur, 148
Life expectancy, 14
Living standard, 12, 111
Ludden, David, 140

Madhya Pradesh, 132
Madras (Chennai), 17, 25, 32, 59, 87, 89, 97, 99–100, 103, 105–108, 111, 158
Madras (province, region), 31, 38, 60–61, 120, 151, 152
Madras Presidency, 120
Mahad movement, 53, 56–57
Maharashtra, 52, 56, 132–133
Malaya, 160
Manjira, 102
Maratha rules, 68–69, 140
Marathwada, 125
Marx, Karl, 20
McAlpin, Michelle, 41
Migration, 5, 10, 17, 36, 69, 91, 93, 96, 104, 137, 140, 147, 150, 153, 168
Monsoon, northeast, 15, 100, 144
Monsoon, southwest, 9, 15, 29, 143
Monsoon, tropical, 2, 3, 5–8, 21–23, 26, 43, 124, 164, 168, 170, 174–175
Monsoon Asia, 22, 90, 173
Moreland, W. H., 13
Mughal empire, 13, 68, 89, 91
Mutha, 103
Mutiny, 68, 73, 89
Mysore, princely state, 30

Narmada project, 117–118
National Green Tribunal, 85
Nehru, Jawaharlal, 116
North America, 3, 37, 171–172
Northern India Canal and Drainage Act of 1873, 79

Odisha, 122, 131
Ostrom, Elinor, 22

Panchayat, 60, 131
Pani panchayat. *See* Panchayat
Partition of India, 74, 113
Pelsaert, Francisco, 13
Pindary, 142
Plague, 94–95
Plantations, 5, 138, 147
Ponds, 11, 36, 58–59, 92
Population growth, 2, 5, 11, 14–15, 22–23, 87, 93, 96, 98, 104, 167–168, 172
Poverty, 2, 4–5, 13, 23, 25, 75, 109, 138, 154, 162, 164
Presidency Banks, 156–157
Property right, 13, 27, 35, 49–50, 76, 79, 81, 96, 130
Public trust, 24, 27, 42, 65, 79, 81–82, 114
Pune, 58, 60, 62, 69, 102–106, 126, 131
Punjab, 72–74, 121–123, 134, 144, 148, 151

Railways, 26, 32, 34, 37, 41–43, 89, 91, 93, 103, 139, 142, 145–146, 148, 154
Rajasthan, 12, 121, 123, 132–133
Ravi and Beas tribunal, 113, 122
Rayalaseema, 120, 123
Reserve Bank of India, 163
Risely, H. H., 48
Rivers, 6, 17, 21, 29–30, 35, 40, 52, 66–67, 70, 72–75, 77, 79, 81, 84–85, 90, 93, 88–100, 102, 104, 113–120, 122, 145, 170
Rudolph, Lloyd I., 75
Russia, 37

Sahel, 173
Said, Edward, 42
Sanitary Commission, 38
Saptagram, 124
Sax, Joseph L., 82
Seasonality, 5, 7–8, 17, 21, 23–24, 87, 90–91, 135, 137–165, 172
Sewage, 76, 94, 96, 100, 109
Singh, Ranjit, 72
Sirhind canal, 74
Slavery, 151
Slums, 61, 94, 109, 111
Soil conservation, 132
Soldiery, 140–143
Southeast Asia, 7, 37
Sprinklers, 122, 133–134
Step well, 12–13
Stone, Christopher D., 83
Storms, 29, 90
Straits Settlements, 160
Supreme Court of India, 65, 82, 84, 121–122
Sustainability, 3, 18, 22–23, 81, 167, 169, 174–175

Tamil Nadu, 30, 51, 121, 132–134
Tanks, 14, 25, 30–32, 40, 46, 51, 56, 59, 93, 97, 100, 103–104, 110, 114–115, 132–133, 170
Thuggee, 142
Times of India, 33

Trade, 17, 41, 71, 90–91, 93, 101, 107, 130, 138–139, 143, 145–146, 148–149, 154–158, 160–161, 163, 168, 171
Tragedy of the commons, 6, 22
Transhumance, 10
Tungabhadra, 29, 120

Unemployment, 5, 13–14, 17–18, 91, 150, 164, 167
United Kingdom, 18, 106
United States, 18, 106
Untouchability (Offences) Act, 1955, 60
Untouchability, untouchable, 45, 47–49, 51–53, 54, 56–57, 59–62, 75
Urbanization, 5, 23, 67, 88, 90, 94, 124, 168

Wage, 8, 12–13, 76, 98, 138–140, 143, 145, 147–148, 150
Water (Prevention and Control of Pollution) Act, 1974, 83
Water, surface, 4, 7–8, 17, 19, 66–67, 69, 76–77, 97, 99–100, 113, 116, 131, 134, 172. *See also* Lakes; Ponds; Rivers; Tanks
Water, underground, 6, 18–19, 27, 30–32, 34–35, 41–43, 67, 70, 76, 79, 88, 100, 111, 114, 123, 127–128, 131, 134, 170. *See also* Wells
Water conservation, 11, 130, 133
Water cooperatives, 131
Water diviner, 123

Water famine, 24, 33, 37, 172
Watershed management, 132–133
Water stress, 18, 24, 79, 113–135, 168, 170, 174
Wells, 70, 72, 74–75, 77, 87–88, 91, 93, 97–103, 105, 107–108, 123–124, 127–128, 130, 132–134, 144. *See also* Water, underground
West Africa, 7
West Bengal, 113, 128
Western Ghats, 29
Wittfogel, Karl, 20
Women, 33, 61, 107, 139, 150, 152

Yarlung Tsangpo. *See* Brahmaputra